THE

PARENT'S GUIDE TO

CHILDREN WITH AUTISM
2ND EDITION

Dear Reader,

As the parent of a child diagnosed with autism or one on the autism spectrum, you may just be starting your journey of learning how to care for your child. Some of you have already had several years of coping with the unique problems of autism, but, hopefully, the ideas and solutions presented in this book will help you to handle even the hardest, most nerve wracking problems.

By learning as much as possible about day-to-day issues and solutions, as well as reaching out to others for advice and support, you can overcome enormous challenges. Along the way you will most likely find abilities and depths in yourself of which you were unaware.

As a pediatrician who has cared for children for fifty years, I have the greatest admiration for parents who meet every parenting challenge with patience and love. Caring for a child with autism or one on the autism spectrum must be one of the hardest parenting jobs there is. We hope this book will help make each day much easier, so there can be many good times, as well as special memories in the years to come.

Charlotte E. Thompson, M.D.

WELCOME TO THE

EVERYTHING

PARENT'S GUIDES

Everything® Parent's Guides are a part of the bestselling *Everything®* series and cover common parenting issues like childhood illnesses and tantrums, as well as medical conditions like asthma and juvenile diabetes. These family-friendly books are designed to be a one-stop guide for parents. If you want authoritative information on specific topics not fully covered in other books, *Everything®* Parent's Guides are your perfect solution.

 Alerts

Urgent warnings

 Facts

Important snippets of information

 **Essentials**

Quick handy tips

 **Questions**

Answers to common questions

When you're done reading, you can finally say you know **EVERYTHING®**!

PUBLISHER Karen Cooper

DIRECTOR OF ACQUISITIONS AND INNOVATION Paula Munier

MANAGING EDITOR, EVERYTHING® SERIES Lisa Laing

COPY CHIEF Casey Ebert

ACQUISITIONS EDITOR Brett Palana-Shanahan

SENIOR DEVELOPMENT EDITOR Wendy Lazear

EDITORIAL ASSISTANT Ross Weisman

EVERYTHING® SERIES COVER DESIGNER Erin Alexander

LAYOUT DESIGNERS Colleen Cunningham, Elisabeth Lariviere, Ashley Vierra, Denise Wallace

Visit the entire Everything® series at *www.everything.com*

THE
EVERYTHING®
PARENT'S GUIDE TO
CHILDREN
WITH AUTISM
2ND EDITION

Expert, reassuring advice to help your
child at home, at school, and at play

Adelle Jameson Tilton
Charlotte E. Thompson, M.D., Editor

A **adams**media
Avon, Massachusetts

To all the special parents and grandparents who
care for children on the autism spectrum

An Everything® Series Book.
Everything® and everything.com® are registered trademarks of F+W Media, Inc.

Published by Adams Media, a division of F+W Media, Inc.
57 Littlefield Street, Avon, MA 02322 U.S.A.
www.adamsmedia.com

ISBN 10: 1-4405-0392-3
ISBN 13: 978-1-4405-0392-4
eISBN 10: 1-4405-0393-1
eISBN 13: 978-1-4405-0393-1

Printed in the United States of America.

10 9 8 7 6 5 4 3 2 1

Library of Congress Cataloging-in-Publication Data
is available from the publisher.

Many of the designations used by manufacturers and sellers to distinguish their products are claimed as trademarks. Where those designations appear in this book and Adams Media was aware of a trademark claim, the designations have been printed with initial capital letters.

This book is intended as general information only, and should not be used to diagnose or treat any health condition. In light of the complex, individual, and specific nature of health problems, this book is not intended to replace professional medical advice. The ideas procedures and suggestions in this book are intended to supplement, not replace, the advice of a trained medical professional. Consult your physician before adopting any of the suggestions in this book, as well as about any condition that may require diagnosis or medical attention. The author and publisher disclaim any liability arising directly or indirectly from the use of this book.

This book is available at quantity discounts for bulk purchases.
For information, please call 1-800-289-0963.

All the examples and dialogues used in this book are fictional, and have been created by the author to illustrate disciplinary situations.

au·tism (ôʹtĭzʹəm) n.

Condition affecting the processing, integrating, and organizing of information that significantly impacts communication, social interaction, functional skills, and educational performance. There are many manifestations and degrees of severity in the autism spectrum.

Contents

Introduction

If you are the parent of a child with autism or on the autism spectrum, you may wonder "Why me, what did I do to deserve this?" There are no good answers to this question despite the fact that more and more children are diagnosed with autism each year.

Instead of focusing on why your child has autism, you will find that life will be much easier and fuller if you can learn to live a day at a time and find creative ways to handle both the daily and the long-term problems. This will leave time for family fun and also time for you.

Practical solutions to seemingly insurmountable problems are provided in the following pages, plus advice on handling family and community difficulties. Autism will change not only your life as a parent, but the lives of other children in the family, the grandparents, and relationships with friends and neighbors. Some family members will be supportive while others will pull away. This can be extremely painful and you will need to find ways to shield yourself and your children. Even a single unkind remark can pierce like a sharp dagger.

The diagnosis of autism is certainly not the end of the world for you or your family. Many brilliant people have been diagnosed with autism and some have done amazing things. The trick is to find a way to unlock the mysteries of your child's brain and channel his abilities into healthy ways of living. Finding a cure or effective treatment is of paramount importance, and you can help others to understand autism spectrum disorders by working for more international research that will benefit everyone.

As parents, you will be an important part of the team you put together to help your child. It is particularly important to first find an autism expert who can guide you through the diagnostic process and the labyrinth of treatments and medications. It may take considerable time and effort to find the right physician to care for your child. Networking with other parents should help you find just the right professionals to be part of your team of experts. You and your child deserve the very best.

If your first visit to a physician leaves you feeling uncomfortable, then keep looking. No doctor or other professional should ever make you feel inadequate. Never forget that when it comes to your child, you are the expert. A good physician will want to learn things from you, as you learn from her. Learn to trust your instincts, and if you have any reservations about a professional, think twice. A professional degree does not necessarily indicate that an individual has compassion, wisdom, or common sense. Along the way remember that not only do you to need to pay attention to yourself and your partner, but also to your other children. Siblings of a child with autism can feel unimportant and left out and will need special times with each parent. It is a juggling act, but if you take time for yourself, get some exercise, try to eat well, and plan time for fun, then you will be able to keep all the balls in the air at once.

The advice and solutions given in this book should help make your days easier and help to keep your life in balance. Then as you solve more and more problems, the realization will come that no matter what lies ahead, you will find a solution and your confidence will continue to grow.

CHAPTER 1

The World of Autism

L earning about autism spectrum disorders is a bit like learning an unfamiliar language. It is a new world, and the customs and behaviors may seem foreign. From the moment you receive the diagnosis, everything changes.

In all likelihood, as a mom or dad, this will not be the parenting experience you had dreamed about. There will be pitfalls and disappointments along the way. However, the good news is that this world can be navigated successfully, and it can be the beginning of something different, full of adventure and the pride of great accomplishment.

What Are Autism Spectrum Disorders?

Often referred to as ASD, autism spectrum disorder is a broad classification of conditions sharing similar signs and symptoms. Many times ASD is referred to as pervasive developmental disorder (PDD) because it involves delays in many areas of development. Historically, ASD has been the more commonly used term in Europe and has recently been accepted as the proper term in the United States. This differs from pervasive developmental disorder "not otherwise specified" (PDD-NOS), which will be discussed in more detail later in this chapter. ASD in its widest definition refers to the class of disorders in which there are several similar symptoms. Each condition within the spectrum has its own label, and there are differences in how each condition is manifested.

Experts believe that all autism spectrum disorders are as individual as fingerprints. No two children with autism display the disorder in exactly the same way. The variety of symptoms and behaviors displayed by children with ASD do certainly bear this out.

Classical Autism

Autism is the most commonly known of the spectrum disorders. First written about in the 1940s by Dr. Leo Kanner, a psychiatrist at Johns Hopkins University, autism was rarely seen by physicians. Characterized primarily by communication and socialization difficulties, classical autism can be a very isolating and frustrating condition.

If your child is diagnosed with autism, chances are you may also hear the diagnosis of PDD. That is because classical autism is also the best known of the pervasive development disorders, rivaled only by PDD-NOS.

Classical autism is a syndrome. A syndrome has signs and symptoms that can be identified as a specific entity. Children with autism will have many similar symptoms, but there may also be differences.

The Signs and Symptoms of Autism

Autism has specific signs and symptoms that may be more prominent in one child than another. Parents must remember that symptoms considered autistic in one child may not present themselves in another child who is also considered autistic. This often makes for difficulty in diagnosis. Without a definitive lab test, a diagnosis of autism can only be made based on evaluation of the symptoms and specific developmental tests. As a rule, most children with autism exhibit specific signs and symptoms that characterize autism spectrum disorders to variable degrees. The following signs and symptoms are not exhibited in all children with autism, but are signs that the condition may exist:

- Expressive and receptive communication deficits and social deficits
- Insistence on routine and resistance to change
- Appearing to be "off in their own little world"
- Resistance to physical closeness such as hugging
- Attachment to "odd" toys such as kitchen utensils
- Parallel play—playing beside other children rather than interacting with them—and lack of imaginative play
- Sudden and apparently unexplainable anger and tantrums
- Repetitive behaviors and obsessive-compulsive disorder
- Splinter skills—excelling in a particular skill that is above the apparent IQ level
- Appearing to experience sensory overload in normal environments

 Essential

The word *autism* originates from the Greek word *autos*, meaning "self." This disorder was named autism because it was believed to be an excessive preoccupation with oneself resulting from a lack of motherly love. This theory has been proved false, and autism is now recognized as a developmental disorder.

The Struggle with Communication

With classical autism there is a marked reduction in verbal communication, or a child may not speak at all. Echolalia is a speech pattern seen in autism spectrum disorders in which a child echoes the words spoken to him. For example, instead of responding to a question with an answer, the child just repeats the question.

Children with autism also have difficulties with nonverbal communication. It is problematic for a child with autism to understand, use, and interpret subtle nonverbal language cues, such as facial expression or tone of voice, and translate these into meaningful language.

The difficulty with communication often accentuates the other deficits in autism. Frustration is a common problem with a child unable to communicate his most basic needs, and the result of frustration is often anger. A child will either struggle to communicate or withdraw even further if he is unable to convey thoughts and feelings to others.

The Problem with Conceptual Thinking

Children with autism also struggle in a profound way with conceptual ideas and thought patterns. For example, a child with autism may associate leaving the house with putting on a coat. Now imagine that same child outdoors without a coat on, and the temperature drops dramatically. Although the child might have a coat with him, even in his hands, he will not put it on. Why not? He associates the coat with leaving the house, not with a solution to cold weather, and the concept of using the coat for protection is nonexistent.

Because of the difficulty the child has in understanding concepts, he becomes limited in many ways. The child does not recognize that other people have their own thoughts, feelings, attitudes, and beliefs, and the child becomes even more isolated.

Anger and Aggression

Although not all children with autism display aggression, it is a very common symptom, and temper outbursts and outright tantrums are common. These can range from a brief explosion to a full-fledged meltdown. Children with autism may also strike out through hitting and/or biting as well as by destroying objects and possessions.

A child with autism throwing a temper tantrum is not a child acting "spoiled" or "bratty." Unfortunately, parents of children with ASD hear these terms quite often. These behaviors are a symptom of a disorder, not a result of poor parenting skills.

PDD-NOS

PDD, as mentioned previously, stands for pervasive developmental disorder; NOS means "not otherwise specified." In real-life terms, this means that the physicians and child psychologists diagnosing a child with PDD-NOS know that the disorder is within the pervasive development category or on the autism spectrum, but does not fit neatly into any particular category. As such, it is classified as a PDD that has no further specification—it isn't quite autism, isn't quite Asperger's, and isn't quite childhood disintegrative disorder (CDD), or any other PDD.

 Alert

If your child has been diagnosed with a PDD, ask the physician or psychologist why this diagnosis was given rather than autism or Asperger's Syndrome. A PDD diagnosis may stand between your child and benefits to which she should be entitled.

PDD-NOS has essentially the same set of signs and symptoms that autism does, but the severity of the symptoms is not as extreme as those found in autism. A child who has PDD-NOS may initiate speech, using language that is appropriate to the context of the social situation. There will be deficits compared to the milestones of normal childhood development; however, they will not be as blatant as in the case of a child who has autism. Echolalia is a less frequent occurrence in these cases and auditory processing skills are more advanced.

Social skills in a PDD-NOS child are also less of a challenge. These children are able to interact at varying degrees with parents, siblings, other adults, and children. Imaginative play may still be limited but interactive play is somewhat more common than it is with a child who is autistic.

Asperger's Syndrome

Dr. Hans Asperger first documented Asperger's Syndrome at the same time Dr. Kanner was writing about autism. Both physicians were unaware of the other's work, as open communication between German and American scientists was not possible during World War II. The two physicians, however, arrived at the same conclusion at a time when ASD had not yet been officially identified. European physicians diagnosed Asperger's Syndrome, and American physicians diagnosed Kanner's Syndrome, which was the name initially given to autism.

It was not until the early 1980s that Asperger's was brought into American diagnostic categories, and it was a full decade later that Dr. Asperger's original paper on the topic was translated into English. It was during the early 1990s that Asperger's Syndrome was placed on the autism spectrum and became a disorder independent of other spectrum disorders. Several signs distinguish Asperger's Syndrome from other disorders on the spectrum:

- Essentially normal speech development with phrases usually used by age three
- Essentially normal cognitive development
- Essentially normal development in self-help and curiosity about the world
- Gross motor skills are often delayed and clumsiness is common
- Eye contact, facial expression, and body language inappropriate to the social situation

- Difficulty establishing and maintaining peer relationships
- Difficulty expressing emotions and relating to others with those emotions
- Intense and persistent interaction or attention to particular subjects, objects, or topics
- Repetitive mannerisms such as flapping
- Insistence on routine

Although the symptoms of Asperger's Syndrome may appear similar to that of autism, the normal development of speech, as well as motor-skill difficulties, distinguish this disorder. Keeping in mind there are varying degrees of severity in Asperger's, it becomes easier to understand why diagnosis of this particular form of a high-functioning ASD may be delayed for many years. There are adults who are just now receiving the diagnosis of Asperger's who had been thought of as odd and eccentric for decades.

 Alert

There is now a possibility that Asperger's Syndrome will be eliminated from the fifth edition of the *Diagnostic and Statistical Manual of Mental Disorders*. If that is done then Asperger's and PDD-NOS will both be placed into the broad category of autism spectrum disorder.

The Subtle Cues of Communication

Much of our society's communication is based on unspoken cues, such as hand gestures, body language, eye movements, and even pauses in conversation. All of these convey emotions and messages that may be subtle, but they are crucial to understanding the meaning of what a person is saying. For a person with Asperger's, however, these nonverbal cues are totally missed, as they live in a literal world where words have only literal meanings.

This socialization impairment is the most obvious symptom of Asperger's Syndrome.

It is possible for people with Asperger's to learn social mannerisms by rote, but they do not generally understand the meaning behind them, and consequently, socialization suffers. Often people will misunderstand what a person with Asperger's is trying to say because his conversation is so literal. These misunderstandings can lead to hurt feelings and anger.

 Essential

> There are children who are extremely shy and take a long time to interact with other children. A child like this could be thought to have Asperger's Syndrome. The difference is that in time, a shy child will begin to make friends and not insist on solitary play. It must be when he or she feels comfortable with interacting.

Asperger's versus Autism

One challenge for parents of very young children is distinguishing Asperger's Syndrome from autism. If the parents have no other children, they may not have a frame of reference for comparison, or they might not realize how different the social world is for children with Asperger's. In addition, if a child is very talkative and seems somewhat advanced in her interests, the parents may think the child is unusually gifted rather than narrowly and persistently focused on a subject, object, or topic.

If you have a child who exhibits the symptoms of Asperger's, it is very important to get an early accurate diagnosis so appropriate intervention can begin. Testing by qualified medical and other professionals can determine where or if your child falls in the autism spectrum and what treatments and therapies should be initiated. As with all disorders on the spectrum, early intervention offers the best hope for a promising future.

 **Alert**

It is not uncommon to hear people with Asperger's Syndrome refer to themselves as "Aspies." This is not a derogatory term, but it should be used only with someone who is close, such as a family member or another child who also has Asperger's Syndrome.

High-Functioning Autism

High-functioning autism (HFA) is a disorder on the autism spectrum that is often confused with Asperger's Syndrome. It is, however, a distinct disorder. There is controversy about HFA because of the standard used to separate it from classical autism.

Today, many autism experts feel that approximately 75% of children with autism are developmentally delayed. However, they also recognize this as a very gray area, in need of further study, with a diagnosis and outcome that is difficult to determine. The technical standard for distinguishing high-functioning autism from classical autism is the presence of developmental delay. In the past, a child with autism who was delayed was considered to have classical autism, and if delay was not present the disorder was diagnosed as high-functioning autism. If your child has a diagnosis of autism, do not assume she is delayed. This may be the farthest thing from the truth.

If a child is nonverbal and is unable to understand concepts, she will perform poorly on a Stanford-Binet test. A score of seventy or below on an IQ test is recorded as developmental delay. However, it is unlikely that a child with autism can be measured accurately with standardized IQ testing. Many physicians and psychologists feel that children with autism are inaccurately labeled as being delayed when given improper tests, which makes the distinction between classical autism and high-functioning autism even harder to determine.

If spectrum disorders could be viewed on a scale, high-functioning autism would fall between classical autism and PDD-NOS. The fine line between HFA and Asperger's lies in the child's motor skills. Although there are always exceptions, children with classical or high-functioning autism will not have the deficits in motor skills that a child with Asperger's displays.

 **Question**

What is IQ?
IQ stands for "intelligence quotient." It is a number derived from a Stanford-Binet test. However, this test should not be used with a child who has language or communication difficulties. Instead, a group of tests known as a "psychometric panel" should be administered by a child psychologist.

Rett Syndrome

This spectrum disorder is unique, as it affects girls almost exclusively. Until recently, it was thought that a male fetus could not survive the disorder, and therefore all Rett Syndrome children were female. Research now shows that although Rett Syndrome is rare in boys, it should not be excluded as a diagnosis just because of gender.

A gene mutation causes Rett Syndrome, and the degree of the mutation determines the severity of the condition. If a boy has Rett Syndrome, he will display the symptoms differently from a girl with classic Rett Syndrome, and therefore DNA testing is required to determine this disorder in boys. Rett Syndrome is a rare condition, affecting only 1 in 100,000 children. The diagnosis of Rett Syndrome is made by the observation of symptoms similar to autism. However, the differences between the two conditions become more apparent as the child ages, due to the dramatic regression exhibited in Rett Syndrome. Indicators of Rett Syndrome include:

- Frequent hand wringing, which is unique to this disorder
- The major milestones achieved as an infant
- Loss of skills and abilities beginning at age two with increase in hand-wringing
- Loss of the ability to walk
- Profound developmental delay
- Social skills decreasing with age

Girls with Rett Syndrome are often misdiagnosed as being autistic when they are very young because of the similarities in symptoms. It is between the ages of five and ten that the differences become apparent. The distinctive hand wringing that is characteristic of the disorder begins to interfere with normal motor functioning, making it difficult to perform simple tasks necessary in the activities of daily living. The child may have difficulty feeding herself, dressing, playing, or engaging in activities typical for any young child.

 Fact

There are gender differences in autism spectrum disorders. Seventy-five percent of children with autism and PDD-NOS are boys. There are ten boys for every girl diagnosed with Asperger's Syndrome. Fragile X and childhood disintegrative disorder are also more prevalent in boys. Girls have Rett Syndrome almost exclusively.

Girls diagnosed with Rett Syndrome, or those with Rett Syndrome but improperly diagnosed as being autistic, will benefit from the same therapies used for other spectrum disorders. Because it is sometimes difficult to get a diagnosis of Rett Syndrome until the child is older, parents should proceed with therapies for children with autism. If the diagnosis of Rett Syndrome is confirmed, parents need to prepare for the physical and mental limitations that will occur as the child matures. Working with your child's strengths and abilities at a young age will ease the issues associated with this syndrome later in life.

Other Spectrum Disorders

There are other less-known disorders in the autism spectrum such as childhood disintegrative disorder, Fragile X Syndrome, hyperlexia, Williams Syndrome, and Landau-Kleffner Syndrome.

 Fact

Fragile X Syndrome is the most common inherited form of developmental delay. The responsible gene was discovered in 1991. This has opened the door for research and a drug trial. Boys with Fragile X Syndrome have long faces, big jaws and ears, and enlarged testes. They may be mildly or markedly delayed.

It is common for physicians and therapists not to commit to the diagnosis of autism or one of its cousins, saying instead that a child is "autistic-like." This is usually reluctance on the part of the physician to deliver a diagnosis. It can be difficult for a physician to tell parents that their child has a disorder that will not disappear over time. It can also be extremely difficult for parents to accept such a diagnosis. Labeling a child with the diagnosis of autism is a stigma for many families, and parents will often be in denial.

A diagnosis of autism can also cause a conflict between parents, with one parent accepting the diagnosis and wanting to start therapy immediately, while the other parent is in denial and refuses to allow treatment. If you are in this situation, it would be important to resolve the issue as quickly as possible. It is important for your child that you push for an accurate diagnosis so that the appropriate intervention can begin.

The journey starts, as poets say, with a single step. The first step is the hardest one to take, but once the journey has begun, each small step will become more sure and certain, and your child's progress will begin to be evident.

CHAPTER 2

Diagnosis: ASD

Receiving the diagnosis of a disorder on the autism spectrum is often the most difficult obstacle you, as a parent, will encounter. As previously mentioned, many professionals are reluctant to make the diagnosis of autism. Many others are not qualified to recognize autism spectrum disorders, and if the symptoms are not dramatic, they may attribute them to a behavioral or psychiatric disorder. It is imperative that a parent be assertive in obtaining an accurate diagnosis if he or she believes some form of autism is present.

Age of Onset

Autism is not discriminating. It affects children of both sexes, and strikes all races and ethnic groups. Virtually all children with autism have the diagnostic signs and symptoms between the ages of two and four. According to the Academy of Pediatrics, children may begin to display the signs of autism between eighteen and twenty-four months. Although some children have qualities that trouble their parents almost from birth, it is more common for a child to develop normally up to about eighteen months and then begin to regress, losing skills already mastered. It is common for children with ASD to have normal speech and behavior patterns for a child of eighteen to twenty-four months and then lose that behavior and speech, retreating into a world that they alone occupy. The website *www.firstsigns.org* is helpful if you have concerns about your child. However, the issue is not so much about the age when signs of autism become apparent, as it is about getting an early diagnosis. A correct diagnosis for a child at a very young age means treatment and intervention are then possible. Early interventions can make all the difference in a child's future. If a child receives therapy and treatments beginning at approximately age two or three, the long-term outlook is much better. The future is also much brighter for the entire family.

The problem is often the failure of parents to realize there is a problem. Parents see their children day after day and may not recognize that their son or daughter is not reaching developmental milestones. This is where the extended family can help by raising the alarm about any issues they perceive with the child. Grandparents are often the ones to spot the delays and may be the first to point them out. Unfortunately, even if a grandparent realizes a grandchild has a problem, this may be unacceptable to the parents and nothing will be done until a teacher or physician insists that the child be tested.

Typical Symptoms

Although each child will display his particular type of ASD in a unique way, there are specific symptoms that form a basis on which a diagnosis can be made. The different degrees of these symptoms will determine the specific diagnosis. Although, for example, almost all spectrum disorder kids will have communication deficits, a classical autism case will display speech issues differently from a child who has Asperger's Syndrome.

ASD is characterized by difficulties in three main areas: social interaction, communication, and patterns of behavior, interests, and activity. Within these three categories are four criteria used to determine if the diagnosis of ASD is appropriate.

A diagnosis of ASD requires that at least one of the signs within each category be met, along with a minimum of six signs from all of the categories.

Children with autism usually display these signs readily. By contrast, pervasive developmental disorder, which is characterized by the same symptoms in milder form, is less easily diagnosed. Parents may need to have consultations with several experts to determine the exact diagnosis in the less extreme cases.

 Fact

The diagnosis of all diseases and disorders in the United States are standardized through manuals on which medical professionals have collaborated in order to achieve uniformity. The *Diagnostic and Statistical Manual of Mental Disorders*, 4th edition, published by the American Psychiatric Association, is the manual used to classify autism spectrum disorders. Wherever a patient sees a physician, the same standards are applied to classify a particular disorder.

Social Interaction

How a child interacts socially is the first of the three categories examined to ascertain whether an autism spectrum disorder is present. The child's physician will be involved, and a child psychologist or psychiatrist may also examine the child or do specific tests. Other experts will be consulted if needed. The professionals will look for:

- Reduction or absence of eye contact, facial expressions, or body language
- Inability to form friendships within a peer group
- Unwillingness or inability to share enjoyment or accomplishments with others
- Inability to relate and share emotions on a social level

The impairment of social skills in a child with autism may be obvious to a parent, even when a child is very young. As a child matures, the interaction skills within the peer group isolate the child further, as he is unable to relate to other children and adults.

Communication

Communication is the second area experts analyze to determine if autism or a related condition is present. This exam involves a physician, speech therapist, and possibly other experts such as a child psychologist or psychiatrist. The communication difficulties in an ASD child are typical to most of the conditions on the spectrum. These include:

- Reduction, absence, or loss of spoken language
- No attempt to replace language with another method of communication
- Inability to converse with another person even if speech is present
- Repetitive use of words, or echolalia (echoing words without meaning)
- Absence of imaginative play typical to a specific age group

 Fact

The behaviors of autism may seem strange, but upon consideration, you will see they reflect the child's effort to establish predictability and order in his world. A world with limited language, or no language at all, is out of control. Repetitive behavior can help the child gain some control.

Communication is imperative for human beings to function successfully. This impairment may be the most painful for parents to understand and cope with on a day-to-day basis. A child may have had language at a young age, perhaps saying "mommy" or "daddy" or identifying various objects within the house, and then lose those words completely.

A child may be suspected of being deaf because of the total lack of response to spoken language. It is common for the diagnostic trail to begin with a parent or grandparent asking for an auditory test because of the child's apparent lack of hearing. However, when the tests show that the child's hearing is normal, further testing will most likely lead to the ASD diagnosis.

Patterns of Behavior, Interests, or Activity

The behaviors in a child with ASD are very distinctive and will be an indicator of where a child places on the spectrum. This exam involves a physician, who may be a pediatric neurologist, a child psychologist, various therapists, and possibly experts in the mental health field. They will look for characteristics such as:

- Intense preoccupation with a particular activity
- Compulsive engagement in routines that serve no practical function
- Repetitive movements such as flapping, spinning, and/or body movements
- Intense preoccupation with parts of a whole—for example, the spinning tires on a bicycle rather than the entire bicycle

 Fact

Some children with autism engage in a behavior called stimming. This stands for self-stimulating behavior, which some experts believe is used as a calming measure. Stimming can include: rocking, spinning an object repeatedly, twisting or twirling an object, repeating words or phrases, and other repetitive activities.

The behaviors of ASD are perhaps the best known of the signs and symptoms. Films have illustrated behaviors exhibited by people on the autism spectrum, so the public is familiar with this set of symptoms. Most children with autism appear perfectly normal to the bystander until certain behaviors such as flapping or spinning indicate that autism or a related condition is present. These behaviors are an early indicator as well, and they may be what prompt parents to seek a medical opinion.

 Essential

The intensely repetitive use of a VCR to watch the ending credits of a film is a common behavior in children with ASD. They will often spend an hour or more rewinding the tape to view the words as they move by on the screen. Music accompanying these credits is even more appealing.

Your Emotional Reaction

When parents first absorb the information that their child is somewhere on the autism spectrum, they experience various stages of emotion as they cope with feelings of grief and loss. You will, too. Never allow anyone to make you feel guilty for experiencing these emotions. There *has* been a loss—a loss of dreams, potential, and hopes for a future that will now be different from any you could have anticipated. You most likely will experience guilt, denial, hopelessness, depression, sadness, anger, desperation, and any number of emotional reactions. All of these reactions are normal.

Loss of Dreams

When a couple learns of a pregnancy, it is almost impossible not to have expectations for the infant growing in the mother's womb. It is also natural to project dreams of this child's future: playing baseball, camping, marching in the school band . . . the list of possibilities is as varied as the families into which the children are born.

When a child is diagnosed with a disability, so many of the preconceived notions of what life could have been like for this child are lost. The feeling of loss is tremendous. It is a devastating blow to parents. The imagined arguments over curfews, borrowing the car, going to college, and bringing home a boyfriend or girlfriend for the first time become anticipated events that just slip away from the future like water through open fingers. This loss of dreams is not unlike a death, and all of the hopes of the future have to be calibrated into a new pattern of thought.

Guilt

Parents invariably turn inward when something goes wrong with their child. It is a natural reaction. As a mother, you may question every aspect of your pregnancy and wonder what you did to cause the autism or what you could have done to prevent it. You may look in the mirror and analyze every moment in an effort to determine what you did wrong to cause this to happen to your child. As a dad, you may also turn inward as you find ways to blame yourself for what has happened—even going so far as to despise yourself for some perceived or imagined wrong.

It is important to understand that ASD is not caused by parental neglect. It is not your fault. It is even more important for health care providers to realize parents are going through this grieving process and that guilt makes the ability to cope with ASD much more difficult.

Denial

When a situation arises that exceeds a person's ability to cope, such as the diagnosis of a terminal disease, denial is often the result. It is human nature to handle a devastating situation by simply pretending it does not exist. This is not a failure on the part of the person to "handle it." In many ways, it shows that the coping mechanisms are functioning normally in the part of the human brain that allows only a certain amount of stress to be processed at a time. By avoiding a stress overload, the ability to cope is maintained.

 Fact

Feeling guilt without reason can have the same effect as excessive stress. Headaches, depression, and other physical and emotional symptoms may be experienced, and harmful activities such as overeating or substance abuse may occur in an attempt to remove the pain. Autism is no one's fault and there should be no blame.

If one or both parents remain in denial, it is important that they seek intervention through some form of counseling. Counseling can help a person understand that while the disability does change a parent's life, it need not ruin the parent/child relationship.

 Alert

Everyone has to cope in her own way. For some, acceptance comes quickly; for others, it is a lengthy process. There is no right or wrong way to do this. Learning to cope with the diagnosis of autism has to be done at your own pace.

Hopelessness

Your ability to deal with the diagnosis of autism will wax and wane. At times you will feel you can handle just about anything; at other times you will feel totally helpless to protect and assist your child. Both of these reactions are normal. There will be many times when you can't make life easier for your child with autism, and feelings of hopelessness will be natural at such times. Just ride it out and remind yourself that tomorrow may be easier.

Many parents look at a child's entire life and, in one day, try to solve all the problems they foresee their child facing. This aggravates the feeling of hopelessness. Time teaches us that problems cannot be solved in one day. It is normal to experience feelings of hopelessness when you cannot easily solve the problems your child faces. Just remember, these feelings will usually pass and if they don't, some counseling could be helpful.

Anger

Hearing that a child has a lifelong disorder with an unknown cause and for which there is no absolute and effective treatment is enough to make anyone angry. Anger is a normal part of loss. Depression is anger turned inward unless it is genetic or has a metabolic basis, so it is important to acknowledge anger and displace it properly.

 Essential

It is not uncommon for one or both parents to get so involved with physicians and professionals once the diagnosis of an autism spectrum disorder is made that they have no other life. This can lead to multiple problems. Every parent must continue to be an individual and get away from the autism world as often as possible.

It is only natural to be infuriated with a situation that is out of your control; learn to be gentle with yourself and your family when you feel angry. Talking it over with a therapist or trusted friend can be very helpful. Meeting other parents who are dealing with the same challenges is also helpful. Support groups are available all over the United States and Canada. Surrounding yourself with people who also have children with autism will help the anger dissipate into actions that are more constructive.

Desperation

This is one of the most common reactions; virtually all parents will experience this emotion. Parents of newly, and not so newly, diagnosed children will do or try just about anything to "cure" ASD. Many spend hours of research on the Internet, in libraries, in public records, or private book collections to find the one thing that may "fix" their child's autism. It is not unusual to find a parent spending six to eight hours each day on the Internet exploring an unfamiliar treatment.

It is important that parents recognize their vulnerability in this area. The tantalizing product that may cure your child is hard to resist. Many unscrupulous people are out there who are more than willing to sell you the latest autism cure for a "reasonable price," never to be seen or heard from again.

Autism Awareness

Over the past few years, there has been considerable debate regarding statistics that show an increase in the number of children diagnosed as autistic or on the spectrum. Has the number of children with autism increased, or has better diagnostic criteria resulted in the appearance of a higher incidence? This question has divided the autism community.

As mentioned earlier, autism was documented for the first time in the 1940s, when it was theorized that "refrigerator mothers," those mothers who withheld love from their children, were causing the syndrome. Because of that, autism was labeled a psychiatric disorder and 50 percent of diagnosed children were institutionalized, forgotten by a society that never knew them in the first place.

Thirty years ago, the incidence of autism was between 1 and 4 per 15,000 children. It was a rare disorder, and few people had ever heard of it. Certainly even fewer had met anyone who had autism.

After 1990

In the recent past, however, the number of children diagnosed with autism has exploded. It is difficult to find exact statistics on autism, but estimates by some research organizations show that it affects anywhere from 1 or 2 children per 150 to 1 per 100. The Centers for Disease Control (CDC) reported that during the 2000–2001 school year, there were more than 15,000 three- to five-year-olds and more than 78,000 six- to twenty-one-year-olds in the United States with autism, as defined by the Individuals with Disabilities Education Act (IDEA). These estimated numbers are lower than the actual count, as students in private schools or home schooling environments are not included.

As autism has increased, the general population with the United States has become more interested. During a prime-time newscast, CNN reported that California—the only state that keeps records on the incidence of autism—had documented an increase of nearly 300 percent. However, the CDC states that the exact number of ASD children in California is unknown, despite the existence of Centers of Excellence for Autism and Developmental Disabilities Research and Epidemiology (CADDRE) in that state.

Better Diagnostics or Legitimate Increase?

The question remains whether the numbers are a true reflection of an increase of actual children with an ASD or if the procedures for diagnosis are simply more accurate now. Could it just be that it is recognized and properly labeled more often because our society has become better educated and therefore more aware of autism and related conditions? Were children who had autism thirty years ago overlooked and therefore not treated? Many parents and researchers find themselves at odds over this point, and the children are in the middle of the debate.

The unanswered question that essentially solves the debate pertains to adults. If autism has not increased in numbers and it is simply being diagnosed more carefully and accurately now, where are all of the adults with autism who were undiagnosed as children? Where are the children with autism who were born forty and fifty years ago?

 Fact

"Medicine for Autism Today," a neuro-immune dysfunction syndrome (NIDS) project, documented a study that illustrated the dramatic rise in cases of autism when they reported a 900 percent increase. Autism, according to this study, is growing faster than any other special-needs disorder in the world. Other studies show a 300 percent increase.

A National Epidemic

If the increase in the ASD population is in fact an increase in the numbers of actual children with ASD. rather than a reflection of better diagnostics, what does this mean for these children and our society? The documentation showing the percentages of chil dren in the autism spectrum is substantial. Regardless of why the numbers are up, the fact is that there are a lot more children with autism, and it is going to affect our society.

Many people do not feel that the word epidemic is appropriate for autism spectrum disorders. Epidemics imply a contagious disease, and although autism and the related conditions are not contagious, they do share other qualities of an epidemic. Strictly defined, an epidemic is an illness or condition that spreads rapidly and affects a large number of people. In common usage, the term implies something that grows unchecked and continues to affect more and more people. Autism certainly fits into that classification.

Possible Causes

Nothing divides the autism community more deeply than a discussion of the potential causes of autism. Perfectly normal and rational adults will come together in meetings and benefits to raise awareness of autism issues and end up in bitter arguments about what causes autism. Many of the disagreements over the cause of autism have been so hostile that the debates themselves have actually overshadowed the main purpose of the gathering—to raise awareness of the disorder itself.

Some organizations have worked hard to achieve unity as the foundation of their structure and have not taken a stand on causes. However, many more have sprung up with the express purpose of catering to what that particular organization and its members have determined to be the trigger of ASD. Disagreements over cause and treatment have divided the autism community as a whole and dealt a near-fatal blow to the autism movement.

 Alert

The most critical problem facing the autism community today is the lack of unity. Without unity, progress cannot be made toward finding a treatment or cure, let alone a cause. The autism community must put aside their differences and work together to help fund and insist on more national research.

To understand why there is such general disagreement, it must be understood that there are some very controversial issues behind autism spectrum disorders. One possible cause that has been advanced is contamination with lead or heavy metals. The conflicts over vaccinations, genetics, disease processes, diets, and allergies, to name a few, have driven deeply into the consciousness of parents of children with autism. It is human nature to want to blame something or someone for a loss, and it is no less true where autism is concerned. Many feel there is no one single cause but that a combination of triggers, combined in a unique way has caused a cascade effect resulting in the condition we call autism and its related disorders.

Neuro-Immune Dysfunction Syndrome (NIDS)/ Autoimmune Disease

Interestingly enough, when the number of autism spectrum disorders in the population began to increase, so did the incidences of autoimmune diseases and chronic fatigue syndrome (CFS), as well as attention deficit disorders (ADD/ADHD). It is common to find a family in which one parent suffers from CFS or another autoimmune disorder, an older child has ADD, and a younger child falls somewhere on the autism spectrum. It is as if something got into the environment of the home and attacked each family member differently based on the individual's age.

The NIDS theory says that many, if not most, patients who suffer from a variety of autoimmune disorders, as well as autism, actually have a neuro-immune dysfunction. This causes chemical imbalances, which subsequently causes a restriction in the blood flow to the brain. In autism, the area of the brain affected would be the area controlling speech, language, socialization, and obsessive behaviors. The trigger for these changes could be environmental, or an illness.

If this theory holds true, then we're dealing with a new disease that has a great potential for treatment. This theory has not yet been proved, but physicians researching NIDS and the treatment of it are seeking to modify or eliminate the symptoms of autism in their patients.

Vaccinations

In 1998, Dr. Andrew Wakefield had an article published in a British medical journal, the *Lancet*, stating he had found a connection between autism and the vaccine for measles, mumps, and rubella. Because of this article that has now been withdrawn and the data declared false, a great many parents have not allowed their children to be immunized. This has resulted in an increase in measles and other diseases and even deaths. Dr. Wakefield has now lost his license in England to practice medicine.

 **Alert**

> If a parent chooses not to have a child immunized, upon entering school, a religious exemption may be claimed or a letter can be presented from the child's physician stating that he believes vaccinations would be harmful to the child's health and should not be given.

It was recently reported that one in four parents link autism to vaccinations. Even though this has been carefully researched and refuted, one in eight parents say they refused at least one vaccination. As we have more unvaccinated children, there could be major epidemics of communicable diseases causing disabilities and even deaths.

Genetics

Many people believe that the cause of autism spectrum disorders will be found to have a genetic basis. The completion of the Human Genome Project will accelerate this line of research. The fact that many families with one child with autism will later have one or more on the autism spectrum has led many to believe that autism "runs" in families. However, the only autism spectrum disorders that have conclusively been proved to be genetic are Fragile X Syndrome and Rett Syndrome. Both of those disorders can be documented by blood work that looks directly at the chromosomes involved, and the genetic mutation can be identified.

 Alert

> There appears to be a genetic basis for some cases of autism. In families with one child diagnosed with autism, there is a 3 to 9 percent chance of a second child being diagnosed as autistic and there is a 30 percent greater possibility of identical twins being autistic as compared with fraternal twins.

Genetics is a field that is vast and uncharted. The Human Genome Project will enable researchers to delve more deeply into this area than was ever before possible, but it is much like looking for the proverbial needle in the haystack. However, with all the genetic research now taking place there could be some real gains made in understanding the genetics of autism.

Environmental Causes

Another theory that either stands alone or works in conjunction with other theories is that environmental issues may have caused autism. The world is now inundated with pollution, processed food, and toxic elements that were not present in past eras. It is conceivable that humanity has caused this syndrome by environmental abuse.

At this time, like all theories, the truth is unknown. It may be that in the past few decades a new environmental agent has triggered a genetic mutation.

 Alert

It is important for parents of any child with an unusual condition or disability to live just one day at a time and not keep looking far into a future that could or could not be dismal. Making the most of each day is an important skill to learn.

Many feel there is no one single cause of autism but that a combination of triggers, combined in a unique way, has caused a cascade effect resulting in the condition we call autism and its related disorders.

Meanwhile, there are no easy answers for parents faced with the diagnosis of an autism spectrum disorder in one or more of their children. Aggressive research continues in an effort to determine what the cause may be so that the most effective interventions can be put in place.

CHAPTER 3

Other Coexisting
Medical Conditions

Although autism presents considerable challenges by itself, other medical conditions often accompany ASD. Some of these conditions can happen to any child, but it is common to think that if any other condition develops, it must be part of autism. Therefore, it's important for the parents of a child with autism to watch closely for symptoms that need medical attention. With the passing years, parents will become more experienced in recognizing problems needing medical care, such as sore throats and headaches.

Tourette's Syndrome

Often, parents of ASD-diagnosed children question whether their child may also have Tourette's Syndrome (TS). TS is a neurological condition characterized by repeated and uncontrollable tics or vocalizations or both. This syndrome is diagnosed symptomatically, as there is no laboratory test to confirm the diagnosis. Signs include:

- Involuntary tics that are impossible to control for any extended period of time
- Tics that appear in repeated and consistent patterns
- Several motor and vocal tics that may or may not appear simultaneously

- Symptoms that occur for more than one year
- Symptoms that increase or decrease in severity over time
- Symptoms that manifest before the age of eighteen or twenty-one, depending on diagnostic criteria

TS was first documented in the nineteenth century by Georges Gilles de la Tourette, a French physician. It is considered a spectrum disorder in itself, with different degrees of severity. Some people with TS have barely noticeable symptoms; others have problems with normal daily activities because the rapid movements associated with this condition interfere to a great degree.

There is controversy and confusion about whether the incidence of Tourette's is higher in children who have ASD, despite the fact that no known link has been proven. Some of the symptoms of Tourette's appear very much the same as the symptoms of autism, thus adding to the confusion. Some confusion also exists in diagnosing TS, because TS and obsessive-compulsive disorder (OCD) are linked and OCD and ASD are also linked.

Coprolalia and Copropraxia

One of the most recognizable symptoms of Tourette's syndrome is coprolalia—the uncontrollable utterance of obscenities. However, this is seen less in children with autism due to their communication issues. It is often combined with a gross motor tic called copropraxia, which is the use of obscene gestures.

Coprolalia affects only 30 percent of patients with TS, although it is the most commonly known symptom of the syndrome. Individuals with this syndrome try desperately to mute the socially unacceptable words but, as with other types of tics, doing so only increases the compulsion. Ultimately, this effort increases, rather than decreases, the behavior.

Anxiety disorders are closely related to TS. The affected person can control the tics to some extent; however, this control comes at great expense. Finally allowing the tics to occur after holding back for a period greatly increases their severity as well as the patient's anxiety. It becomes a vicious cycle as the patient seeks to control the tics for social acceptablilty. When control is lost, the tics become more dramatic. This increases the anxiety, which aggravates the tic disorder.

 Fact

Tics are the involuntary movements that can occur anywhere on a person's body, although the face, neck, and shoulders are the most common locations for tics. Uncontrollable sounds made by a person are called vocal tics and can be very disturbing to others and embarrassing for the person uttering them.

Autism and Tourette's Syndrome

For a child to be correctly diagnosed, it is important to determine if the child has autism and Tourette's or if his tics may be due to autism alone. Many children with autism have a series of tics that appear to be out of their control. With the repeated rhythm and compulsion to act out these tics, it is easy to confuse the two syndromes, but the compulsive aspects of autism are enough to cause this behavior.

If a child with an ASD has TS as well, it can be treated with various medications. However, medications should only be used if necessary, and a definite diagnosis is needed before such medications can be prescribed. A qualified physician should determine the specific diagnosis and prescribe treatment for the disorder.

Obsessive-Compulsive Disorder

Obsessive-compulsive disorder (OCD) is a psychiatric disorder separate from autism, although all disorders on the autism spectrum show some degree of OCD, and studies have shown that the two are closely linked. If a child has ASD, it is very likely she will have an element of OCD as well. OCD symptoms can be quite debilitating and may include the following:

- Thoughts and images that are recurring and persistent
- Anxiety, sometimes severe, resulting from the thoughts and images
- Thoughts and images not normally experienced by most people
- The realization that these thoughts are irrational but an inability to stop them
- Behaviors such as counting, hand washing, or any number of activities done repetitively
- Behaviors that are compulsive and produce anxiety if not performed
- Compulsive behaviors not linked in any rational way to the anxiety they are intended to reduce
- Obsessions and compulsions that interfere with a person's daily activities because of the amount of time they involve

 Fact

Historically, OCD was considered a mental illness, and people with OCD had been treated by psychiatrists. Recent research is beginning to cast doubt on this classification, and alternative avenues of treatment, including behavior modification, have been recommended to people suffering from this condition. It is known that family influences or social pressures do not cause OCD and that a person does not compulsively count things because of a parent's insistence on perfection.

The Prevalence of OCD

OCD is equally prevalent in males and females and does not discriminate based on race, economic status, or ethnic background. Although it usually begins in the adolescent or young adult years, in many cases it begins in childhood.

The National Institute of Mental Health estimates that between 2 and 3 percent of the population in the United States has OCD. That means that over 3 million people between the ages of eighteen and fifty-four have the disorder. OCD accounts for six percent of the total mental health care expenses.

Current research indicates there is a strong possibility that OCD is caused by a misfiring or "mis-wiring" in the brain. Given the close link between TS and OCD, it is also possible that there is a genetic link. Many people with OCD report having a parent who also had it.

OCD with Other Conditions

In a person with another condition, it is often difficult to distinguish OCD from the original problem. This is particularly true with an ASD. Autism by its very nature includes obsessions and compulsions as part of the matrix of symptoms. For example, children with ASD will compulsively put objects in a line, insist that things are ordered in a certain way, and demand that a certain routine be followed. They will become anxious and belligerent if these behaviors or routines are interrupted.

 **Question**

Why does my child line up objects on the floor?
There are many theories why lining up objects is an almost universal symptom in autism. It is an obsession and a compulsion and if lines are disturbed, it is extremely frustrating to the child. It may be a child's attempt to establish order during times of sensory overload.

If your child is diagnosed as having OCD and is not diagnosed on the autism spectrum, it is important that you seek a second opinion if you feel autism may be a possibility. If autism is present, even high-functioning autism, and early intervention is not provided, your child may lose the tremendous potential for advancement at a young age. Don't hesitate to follow your own instincts regarding your child's health. A pediatric neurologist, developmental pediatrician, or child psychologist familiar with autism are all resources that you should consider.

Depression

Depression may occur in children with ASD, especially in older children with Asperger's, due to the sense of isolation and frustration that accompanies their social and emotional issues. Depression may also occur after a severe injury or shock, or due to an underlying genetic or metabolic condition. The symptoms of depression are: sleep disturbance, loss of interest in family, friends, or outside activities, loss of energy, decease in appetite, and little interest in personal appearance.

Whatever the reason for the depression, there are treatment options available, including appropriate medications, counseling, or a good support group. Phototherapy also seems to help some individuals as do exercise and a good diet. If private therapy is not financially possible, some community clinics offer therapy. Teaching hospitals, too, usually have clinics that offer a sliding fee scale.

Bipolar Disorder

An individual with bipolar disorder has moods that swing from one extreme to the other. This disorder is being diagnosed more frequently, either because the condition is more known, and therefore easier to diagnose, or because of other unknown factors.

Some children with autism have bipolar-like symptoms due to hyperactivity, talking rapidly, or repeatedly changing from subject to subject. These symptoms may not necessarily indicate bipolar disorder; however, rapid mood swings in any child should always be brought to the attention of a child psychiatrist who can make the diagnosis. Some of the new medications used to treat this disorder can be extremely effective in controlling these mood swings. However, no child or teen should be started on medication without a complete physical examination, basic blood tests including a complete blood count, and a thyroid panel. A urinalysis should also be part of the diagnostic testing.

Seizures

Of all the conditions that can occur with autism, perhaps none is as frightening to parents as seizures. Parents feel out of control and fearful if their child has seizures. It may be more frightening because most seizures in children with autism do not begin until puberty, so the family has not become accustomed to handling them. However, seizures are not as common as many parents fear; it is estimated that 25 to 30 percent of children with autism will have a seizure disorder.

 Alert

Parents and caretakers must know what to do if a seizure occurs. Dangerous objects need to be removed from the area near the child and parents should check that the child's airway is clear and no food or any object is stuck in her throat. A call to 911 should always be made in case oxygen is required.

Since the seizures most commonly begin at puberty, and hormones become quite active at that time, researchers are looking for the connection between hormones and chemicals within the brain.

Hearing and Auditory Response

A child with an ASD can have visual or hearing disorders just like any other child. The problem for parents and the child's physician is recognizing if a problem exits, Hearing losses may be discovered more quickly in an ASD child because the child's early lack of communication or failure to respond may lead you to suspect that the child is deaf.

It is normal for children to turn their heads to acknowledge their name or to look in the direction of a voice or an interesting sound. Children with autism do not always respond to voice, and this may be your first sign that "something is wrong." It is common when this happens for parents, and especially grandparents, to question whether or not the child can hear. If this happens, the first thing to do is arrange to have the child tested by a qualified specialist.

 Alert

Frequent ear infections that are not properly treated can lead to a loss of hearing. If a physician repeatedly prescribes antibiotics for ongoing ear infections, it would be wise to check with a pediatric ear-nose and throat doctor. An incision to release the pus may be needed so hearing loss does not occur.

Hearing tests are very accurate, even on very young children if they are performed in a pediatric hearing center by experienced audiologists. Audiologists use special equipment to rule out hearing loss. If it is determined that there is a deficit in hearing, the next step will be to determine what kind of deafness is occurring and how to treat it. If a child has a hearing loss, whether total or partial, it is important to intervene with the appropriate hearing aids, even if the child is completely nonverbal. Speech therapy is an important part of the treatment for a child with ASD, but a child must hear properly to learn to integrate speech into his or her life. If the child has difficulty hearing, it will be even more difficult to compensate for the lack of speech and find other ways to communicate.

 Essential

Sign language is the communication tool for the deaf. Although American Sign Language (ASL) is most commonly used, it is not the easiest for an ASD child to learn, as it is very conceptual. Exact Sign Language is more suitable for the way the autistic brain works.

The Importance of Early Diagnosis

It may be difficult for the parents of a deaf child with autism to get an early diagnosis due to the challenge involved in recognizing the symptoms of autism, which are often masked by the hearing impairment. If you have a child with a hearing impairment, but recognize many of the symptoms on the autism spectrum, it is very important to have an evaluation done to determine if autism is also present. Early intervention and therapy is critical, and in the case of a deaf child with autism, therapy must be initiated not only for the hearing loss but also for the autism to ensure the most promising outcome.

The deaf child who has not been diagnosed as being on the autism spectrum will have difficulty with socialization skills, and therapy will be much more difficult. The inability of the child to make eye contact will likely be treated as a behavioral issue rather than as a disorder. The situation can become very stressful for the family when a child is perceived as uncooperative or belligerent; meanwhile, the child is forced to wander about alone in the imposed exile of autism.

There are not many profoundly deaf children who are also autistic, but it does happen. The Rose F. Kennedy Center for Research in Mental Retardation and Human Development did a study on forty-six children with deafness and found that nearly half of those children were also autistic, but had not been diagnosed. The children's progress was suffering severely due to lack of proper intervention. Therapy must be initiated not only for the hearing loss but also for the autism to ensure the most promising outcome.

Sensory Integration

Therapists teaching a deaf child with autism to communicate will use several different approaches to increase communication skills. Perhaps one of the most important therapies for a child with autism is sensory integration, or teaching a child how to work with all of the stimuli that enter into the brain through the senses.

A child with autism can be hypersensitive to sensory input or she can be completely hyposensitive. It depends on where she is on the spectrum, and what impairments she has. The purpose of sensory integration therapy is to train, or "retune," the brain to understand how the different stimuli fit together into a cohesive whole.

 Alert

As the parent of a child with autism, you need to remember that your child may be watching you at any time. You can use these times to teach your child the activities of daily living, but be aware that your child may also see things that could be harmful, such as watching you take medicine.

When a child with autism also has a hearing loss, one of the senses has been deprived of input. It is a myth that the other senses will become stronger to make up for the loss; it only seems that way because people come to depend more on their other senses.

A therapist specializing in sensory integration will help a child who is both deaf and autistic use her visual ability. This is usually done through the use of sign language, which helps place a "visual sound" in the child's mind. This can then be integrated with the other senses, such as taste, smell, and touch.

If your child has a hearing loss as well as autism, you should understand that her progress will be slow, but there will be progress. The challenges will be great, but the victories will be greater. If you are using sign language and are discouraged because you believe your child never looks at you and there isn't any point to continuing, remember that people with ASD visualize in different ways. Your child may have been watching you in her peripheral vision and learned more than you realized.

Hypersensitivity to Sound

Another common problem for children with ASD is hypersensitivity to sound. It is not unusual to see a child who is autistic suddenly cover her ears in an effort to block out all sound. One theory for this hypersensitivity is that people with autism do not discriminate sounds, but hear all sounds equally. As you are reading this book, you are most likely aware of surrounding sounds; traffic on the street, the hum of a heater or air conditioner, a radio, a dog barking in the distance, or any of the normal sounds of life. If this theory is correct, children with autism hear all of these sounds with equal intensity. This could certainly cause a sensory overload!

 Fact

If your child suddenly covers her ears and looks for a way to escape, make every effort to lower the sound level or remove her to a quieter place. Sensory overload is painful, and not relieving the situation may result in an anger outburst or meltdown.

Whether it is not enough sound or too much sound, hearing is an issue for a person with an ASD. This sense is a vital part of functioning in the world, and a child needs to learn how to manage it. Appropriate therapy, especially sensory integration therapy, is vital to success in this area.

Vision Problems

Parents generally will look for vision problems by observing how their child watches television, colors pictures in a coloring book, or gauges distance while playing. A child with autism will most likely do these things in the same manner as other children, so the unique visual problems of a child who has an ASD may be missed.

Identifying the Problem

Most children with autism have some kind of visual problem. Common indications for visual difficulties include:

- Lack of eye contact
- Staring at objects, especially spinning items such as wheels
- Momentary peripheral glances
- Side viewing
- Scanning objects quickly
- Difficulty maintaining visual contact with an object or person
- Crossed eyes (This could also be caused by a muscle imbalance that is correctable. It must be detected before a child is six so the vision in one eye is not suppressed resulting in a blind eye.)
- Eye movement abnormalities

Vision problems occur more often in patients with sensory disorders than in the normal population. When a child has autism, schools, parents, and caregivers often attribute behaviors to autism when visual problems are the actual culprit. Combined with the problems a child with autism has of integrating visual input with other sensory input, this can lead to difficulties that are very hard for the child to overcome.

For example, a child with autism might have difficulty integrating central vision with peripheral vision, leading to less efficient processing by the brain of visual stimuli. This will in turn overlap into other areas and may interfere with motor, cognitive, and speech skills. If you suspect any of these problems, have your child examined by a pediatric ophthalmologist to rule out other reasons for the visual difficulties.

 Essential

One easy way to determine if a child is having visual processing problems is to observe how he watches television. Is his face pressed sideways to the screen and are his eyes rotated, looking for a better angle? If so, an eye exam by a pediatric ophthalmologist is needed.

Vision therapy is a specialized and controversial area of eye care. The specialists who practice in this field are known as developmental optometrists. These doctors perform vision exams and check for particular vision conditions. They can prescribe special lenses that are said to help with the integration of a child's vision and they can prescribe therapies they say will improve vision and sensory integration skills. These therapies are said to be important to maximize the potential of a child's vision, possibly avoid surgery, and alert parents to any eye diseases that require an ophthalmologist. Because vision therapy is controversial, parents should discuss it with an autism specialist and a pediatric ophthalmologist to be sure your time and money is not being wasted.

Visual Processing

Visual health is important, but just as important is visual processing. If a child on the autism spectrum cannot process the information he receives through sight, the entire chain of sensory skills will not be in proper working order. The potential effects of poor visual processing can be multiple. A child might have attention-span problems, an inability to recognize objects from different angles, and further delays in speech and sensory skills.

The likely visual abnormalities in children with autism can cause a total distortion in how they view the world and how they process that information. It can give a child the feeling that objects bounce or swim, jump unpredictably, are fragmented into tiny pieces, or are overly large. Poor visual processing will contribute to problems with fine motor skills, attention deficits, and a variety of social interaction issues. In order for a person to function as a whole, integrated human being, sensory integration must be functioning, and that begins with vision.

Other Physical Challenges

Some physical issues that accompany ASD are a part of the complex picture of the disorder. Conditions such as encopresis, a bowel disorder characterized by leaky stool, and eczema are common in children with ASD. If your child has leaking stool, be sure that she has a rectal examination. Sometimes a child can be so constipated that stool leaks around a hard ball of stool in the rectum. There could also be a problem with the tightness of the rectal or bowel sphincter so this needs to be checked.

It is common for children in the autism spectrum to have abnormal reactions to sensations, such as the apparent inability to feel pain or an intolerance to heat or cold. Clumsiness or gross motor skill issues are common in Asperger's Syndrome patients. Rett Syndrome has its own set of physical issues that can result in the loss of the ability to walk.

Fact

A child with autism is just as likely to break a bone, require stitches, skin a knee, or be subject to any of the childhood injuries that occur to active children of all ages. Having autism will not make these injuries worse or lengthen recovery time.

Any of the physical issues that may occur in a child, including the usual childhood diseases, are just as likely, or as unlikely, to occur in the child with ASD. Migraines, allergies, scoliosis, and any number of disorders occur just as frequently in children with autism. It may be harder for a parent to determine the degree of illness, or even if it exists, due to the communication difficulties and the atypical reaction to pain in the child with autism, but time and experience will teach parents how to resolve these difficulties.

Other Mental Challenges

ASD is characterized by deficits in mental functioning. The most difficult associated problem is developmental delay. Statistics vary widely on how many ASD children are delayed—the estimates range from 30 to 80 percent. Because of the difficulty in obtaining accurate IQ scores in these children, it can be hard to determine if a child is delayed.

Because there is such a wide variance in the estimates of developmental delay for ASD children, it is an area of great concern and controversy. There is no "standard" delay seen in ASD children, which means it may vary from mild to moderate or even to profound delay in some individuals. The more moderate the level of delay the harder it is to determine if it exists at all. Potentially, what seems like developmental delay in some children might be attributable to other symptoms of autism.

Developmental delay is difficult for most parents to accept. They may accept a diagnosis of autism more easily than a diagnosis of delay in their child. Be aware that many people with autism have extraordinary skills in a few areas. These are known as splinter skills and include such things as the ability to determine the day of the week of any given date in any year. Splinter skills are remarkable feats of intelligence in very narrow areas. Having them, or not having them, does not indicate delay one way or the other.

 Essential

> A variety of physicians and therapists should be involved if developmental delay is suspected. A pediatrician with special training in autism is the best physician for the primary care of children with autism, but a child psychologist or child psychiatrist, child neurologist, and a variety of therapists should be involved as well. A team approach will provide the best outcome.

There are no easy ways through the difficulties associated with ASD. Children on the autism spectrum may have multiple problems of varying degrees. One child may have virtually no other physical or mental problems and another might have several. Most children fall in between and have a few problems along with autism.

The most important thing a parent can remember is that not all of this will happen at once, and not all of it has to be solved immediately. It is a matter of discovering the issues, determining the best course of action, and then beginning to walk the path. Your goal? Help your child with autism to become the happiest person possible.

CHAPTER 4

Behaviors

Behaviors that are out of the ordinary are the primary symptom in autism spectrum disorders such as Asperger's Syndrome. The behaviors in ASD are specific to the disorder, and although each child is unique in how he displays autism, certain behaviors are common. Some of these behaviors will interfere with daily life and others will not. Some can be controlled while others are just a part of the pattern of behavior of a particular child.

Obsessive-Compulsive Behaviors

Many behaviors fall into this category, but OCD does not have a consistent pattern. A child with autism may have obsessive and compulsive behaviors such as:

- Lining up objects, such as trains, blocks, cars, or DVDs
- Opening or closing doors on cupboards, closets, or doors to the outside
- Spinning in circles or walking in a circle
- Hand or arm flapping
- Rocking the body back and forth
- Counting objects repeatedly for no apparent reason
- Hiding or hoarding objects

- Preoccupation with objects being placed in a chosen location
- Gestures and facial movements that resemble Tourette's Syndrome
- Narrow food preference, often based on color or shape

These behaviors have two parts; the first part is the obsession with uncontrolled and unwanted thoughts. Because people with autism are either nonverbal or have limited verbal ability, it is difficult to know if those thoughts are present, particularly in children. The second part manifests as compulsive behaviors, which parents, teachers, and professionals can readily see.

Lines

Some experts believe that the creation of lines, and the act of lining up objects, is an attempt by a child with autism to create a sense of order to what he perceives as an out-of-control and disordered world. The sensory overload that is experienced by children with autism also makes this behavior easy to understand; lines are orderly and creating them provides a measure of control.

As explained in the last chapter, it is believed that individuals with autism lack the discriminatory ability to separate environmental auditory input. In other words, when the television is on, the air conditioner is running, the dog is barking, and the phone is ringing at the neighbor's house, a child with autism will perceive the sounds as all being of equal weight.

The same analogy can be applied to other senses as well. Sensory overload is a common problem for children with autism. It is easy to deduce that this "equal opportunity stimuli" would apply to visual input as well. In that case, if the visual part of the brain is on overload, lines are the perfect solution. A line is the shortest distance between two points and that makes it clean and uncluttered. Lines may not be a meaningless compulsive behavior but a way of coping with sensory overload through an order that is understandable and natural for your child.

 Essential

Some parents discourage the creation of lines, resulting in frustrated and irritable children. Other parents allow the behavior, as it seems to reduce stress and anger. The negative aspect to line creation is that preoccupation and absorption may result. If that occurs, divert your child's attention to other activities.

Medications

Parents of children with autism are divided on the use of medications, particularly for controlling behavior, as opposed to treating seizures or other medical conditions. One of the classes of medications used for the compulsive behaviors of autism is known as serotonin reuptake inhibitors (SSRIs). This group includes Zoloft for ages six and above, Luxor for those eight and older, and Paxil, Serzone, and Prozac for those eighteen and above.

SSRI medications used by patients with autism have been shown not only to reduce compulsive behaviors, but also to aid in other symptoms of autism. Most notably, eye contact improves, social interaction becomes easier, the narrow field of interests grows, and the isolation problems manifested by many children with autism decrease. Tantrums and anger are also reduced with the use of SSRIs. The primary symptom of being withdrawn and preoccupied and preoccupation within their own world is also lessened, and the medications have a calming effect.

Side effects include dry mouth, insomnia, and paradoxically, impulsive behavior. These side effects can sometimes be avoided by starting with very small doses and working up to a dose that provides control. These medications are not recommended for people who have seizures or heart problems, so a consultation with a physician who is well acquainted with these medications is prudent.

 Alert

A child must have a complete physical examination as well as a blood panel and urinalysis before any medication is prescribed. Some physicians, particularly psychiatrists, will prescribe medications without being sure that a thorough physical examination and workup have been completed. As a parent you must not allow this to happen.

Routine

One way that obsessive-compulsive behavior manifests in a child with autism is through his insistence on routine. A sudden change in the daily routine, or even a small aspect of that routine, can cause a perfectly good day to go downhill fast. Routine is an important characteristic of autism, and although flexibility can be taught to a certain degree, the need for routine will never disappear completely. Children with autism depend on that routine to know what is going on, what is expected of them, and what they can expect from others.

 Fact

When the parents of a child with autism are separated or divorced, the child may have behavioral problems with the noncustodial parent during visits. This can lead to questions about the ability of a parent to care for the child. In reality, it is the change in routine that is to blame.

If your child is sensitive to routine changes, minimizing the shock of the change is a wise idea. Sometimes sudden change cannot be avoided, so all a family can do is remember how upsetting those changes are to a child with autism. When an unexpected event causes a routine change, such as a snow day for which school is cancelled, distract your child with a good movie or a favorite toy. For the most part you will have to ride it out; it is just one of those things that everyone will have to learn to handle.

Flapping

Flapping is a behavior that can be considered a form of compulsive activity. It is common in all spectrum disorders, but is particularly prevalent in autism. It is something that appears around the time of other autism symptoms and is linked to either strong physical actions or emotional activity. Flapping is a rapid and repetitive hand and/or lower arm motion that resembles waving. It is often one of the first symptoms that parents notice, as it is an atypical behavior in children.

 Question

Is flapping always an indication of autism?
No. While flapping may be one of the earliest symptoms of autism, it is common for some babies to engage in this behavior. However, as a child matures, flapping should disappear. If a child at the age of eighteen months to two years continues flapping, it is something to investigate.

Expressing Excitement

When a child with autism becomes excited, it is common to see this excitement manifested as flapping. Many children will be watching a television program or movie and become so excited that the emotion has to spill out; flapping will be the result. Positive emotions such as excitement, joy, or utter delight are more commonly associated with flapping than negative emotions. Flapping can often herald a loss of control and should be watched and regarded as a signal. Most of the time, flapping means nothing more than the emotion it is connected to, but if an emotion is getting too extreme, flapping will usually precede it.

There are times when a child who is irritated or upset will flap. Parents will see a different "character" to this kind of flapping and will learn to recognize that anger or aggression may be building. This is something that only experience can teach. Learning to correctly anticipate behaviors is part of parenting a child with autism. As the months and years go by, it becomes much easier to do this, so learn to trust yourself, as no one knows your child as well as you do.

Flapping is also seen in children with autism during physical activity. Most children will pump their arms while running. Children with autism will often not pump their arms but will flap while they run. This is related to the activity and not to any particular emotion.

Other Repetitive Behaviors

Flapping isn't the only repetitive behavior that appears in autism. Autism also causes other behaviors that are unique to the disorder. Such actions as twirling, rocking, head banging, facial contortions, eye movements, and unusual voice patterns are also repetitive stereotypical behavioral patterns. These behaviors are different from tics and other repetitive motion disorders, so a diagnosis of autism cannot be based on the appearance of these behaviors alone.

 Fact

Head banging in children who have autism is not unusual. Children not diagnosed as autistic will also sometimes be head bangers as small children. The reason for the head banging is unclear. The most important thing is to be sure your child does not hurt herself.

Behaviors such as head banging and facial contortions are greatly disturbing to parents. These are behaviors that indicate a child has a problem that might need professional help.

Treatment

Professionals have different views on the treatment of flapping and related behaviors. The vast majority feels that if the movement patterns do not respond to the usual medications, no further treatment will be effective. SSRIs, Ritalin, and Risperdal are some of the medications used to treat patients with autism, but there are now many new medications in use. A good website listing these medications is: *www.child-autism-parent-cafe.com/autism-medication.html.*

Apart from drug therapy, the best way for parents to handle unusual movements or behavior is to ignore them. It is unknown why people with autism engage in these behaviors but they seem to fulfill a need. Interrupting them will only cause agitation, which can develop into aggression and anger. Trying to stop these behaviors will be stressful for both parents and child.

Anger and Aggression

Unfortunately, the behavior that is most commonly seen in autism is anger, expressed through aggression, tantrums, and outbursts. Meltdowns are an extreme display of anger. (See Chapter 6 for a more detailed discussion of meltdowns.) Of all of the issues in autism affecting parents, dealing with their child's anger is probably the most difficult.

Anger is caused by frustration, and frustration is an emotion prevalent in children with autism. When communication is difficult or impossible, it is only natural to become frustrated. Consider how you would feel if you were trying to explain something important to someone who does not speak your language. As you attempt to convey your thoughts that are not being understood, your frustration grows; you feel upset and frustrated with the situation and yourself. If you consider that feeling in a child, the only outlet is anger, especially if the child does not have normal social interaction.

Getting Aggressive

Aggression is often the first indication of anger and children with autism are often aggressive toward others. They can also be aggressive with pets, toys, and household items. Keeping in mind the frustration a child feels when he is unable to convey his needs and wants, it is easy to understand why he might turn to whatever method will work to have those needs met. Any child, even one who is successfully learning the social graces of our culture, will become pushier than normal as he struggles to have his needs satisfied. But a child with limited social skills will turn to whatever behavior is successful, and often that behavior is aggression. Anyone and anything can be on the receiving end of the seemingly rude and thoughtless behaviors that can occur as a child with autism strives to get his own way.

 Alert

The medication Risperdal and several others are used to control aggression and anger in children with autism. Parents should watch for side effects such as excessive weight gain and facial tics while their child is taking different medications. Any side effects should be immediately discussed with your child's physician.

Tantrums and Outbursts

It is also common for a child on the autism spectrum who doesn't get his own way, to show anger in the form of an outburst or tantrum. When the child is prevented from having what he wants at any given moment, he may hit or slap without any warning. Parents, siblings, teachers, and caretakers are the usual targets of retaliation. For example, if your child wants a particular toy, or to play with something denied him, he may strike out in anger by hitting or biting.

It isn't unusual for the family dog or cat to bear the brunt of a child's lashing out. He may also throw or break things, which only makes the situation worse, as the child then becomes distressed over the broken item. The child has difficulty gaining control over this repeating cycle. Tantrums and outbursts can end as quickly as they began or may take some time to wind down.

Responding to Aggression

When a child explodes in anger, parents have to think on their feet. This isn't a problem you can analyze and try to solve—you do need to reflect on the issue that brought the anger about for the sake of prevention, but the tantrum or outburst you are seeing has to be dealt with now.

 Question

My child is very angry. What do I do?
It is difficult to know how to react to a child who is out of control, but don't get mad. Try to determine what is frustrating your child, but if that isn't possible you can do little other than prevent damage to your child. Wait it out. It will pass.

It is better to resolve the problem quickly, even if it means giving in to your child's tantrum. It is always unacceptable for a child or adult to strike another person for any reason, at any time. This is the lesson you must convey. You will have an easier time teaching this to your child, if you understand the cause of the outburst.

Many parents resort to punishment if a child loses control over an unmet need that is important, but the situation will only get more out-of-control if the child is punished. If your child has lost control over an inability to communicate some pressing need, his frustration will only increase if he is punished, and the tantrum will escalate. There is enough of a problem with communication without your child feeling that you are punishing him for his attempts to let you know what's on his mind.

Elopement—The Escaping Child

Elopement is something almost all parents of children with autism have experienced at one time or another. Elopement in connection with autism means that the child escapes from home and wanders off alone. It makes for sleepless nights and jittery nerves.

Take the time to view your house as your child would. How can you prevent elopement?

- Put extra locks on all doors that open to the outside.
- Install a security system that monitors people entering and leaving.
- Buy an alarm that will hang on doors to use when away from home.
- Get a service animal (a dog is most useful for this problem).
- Establish a routine: The child never leaves the house unsupervised.
- Inform trusted neighbors of the possibility of elopement.
- Notify the local police department of the possibility of elopement.

There are other things you can do to promote your peace of mind as you protect your child's safety. A large family can work in shifts so that someone always has an eye on the child with autism. If Mom can't cook dinner or even escape to the bathroom for a few minutes, stress levels will rise and tempers will get shorter. The entire family must work together to lessen the stress on each family member.

One solution that will work for any individual with autism, regardless of age or size, is a double-keyed dead bolt. A key is required on either side of the door to lock or unlock this type of dead bolt. If you choose this method, the most important habit to develop is to have a key with you at all times! Put a chain around your neck with the key and have a key well hidden near the door. If a fire should break out, having a double-lock dead bolt can turn a safe situation into a deadly trap.

Having your child wear an identification bracelet is one of the easiest, and most important, steps parents can take. MedicAlert sells an inexpensive bracelet that can be engraved with your child's name, address, and telephone number. Anyone calling the Medic Alert number, 1-800-423-6333, will reach a physician and specific information will be available about your child. Above the child's name have printed "Nonverbal Autistic" or "Limited Verbal Autistic" so that people are immediately aware of the child's situation.

 Fact

Children with autism usually outgrow the elopement problem, but there are children who never do. They are fortunately in the minority. It is unclear if they simply lose interest or if they realize the level of danger, but the important thing is that this is probably not a life sentence.

Special Considerations

If you live near any potentially dangerous situations, such as water or a busy road, it is imperative you have a locking safety system even if your child is not prone to elopement. All it would take is one escape, and a child with autism could easily drown or be hit by a car. Children with autism have been known to walk right in front of a moving car because they lack the ability to understand danger.

It is also wise to contact the city government for the town in which you live so that special road signs can be placed on both ends of your street to send a warning to drivers. It is wise to request a sign that says either "Disabled child at play" or "Deaf child at play." The sign for deafness is the most efficient, as drivers will then be aware that a child may be unaware of them. A sign that says "Child with autism at play," although accurate, can be less than helpful due to the lack of knowledge among the general public regarding autism.

 Essential

If you buy an identification bracelet, be sure to purchase one with a secure fastener. It should be made of stainless steel and have enough links on it to grow with your child. Put it on your child's nondominant hand so it won't interfere with her daily activities.

One of the most frightening forms of elopement can occur in the car. Without the realization of danger, a child with autism may open a car door while the car is moving. Always have your child safety-belted, and place her in a car seat if she is under sixty pounds.

Many of the newer cars automatically lock when the car is started. If your car doesn't have this feature, take it to a mechanic or dealer to have the inside door handle removed on the child's side. In the case of an accident or other emergency, it is important that the other side of the car can quickly be exited. If you can't find anyone to remove the handle, remove it yourself with a wrench and hammer. The cost of the repair, if you wish to have it replaced, is insignificant compared to the tragedy of a child opening the door and falling out of a moving car.

Rental Housing and the Law

Laws provide for reasonable accommodation for a disabled person in rental housing. If you have a child who elopes, or escapes, it is your right to have locks installed on the inside of doorways that the child is unable to open. For younger children, consider installing slide bars placed out of reach. If you have an older child, request a keyed dead bolt. One trick that works well with a slide bar is to place it slightly out of alignment; the door handle then has to be lifted slightly, and a younger child is unable to manage this on his own.

 Fact

Even if a child cannot escape through a window, it is possible that things you own will escape quite easily. Children with autism are still children, and there seems to be great entertainment in throwing items out of windows. Be sure your screens are adequate to keep bugs out and appliances in!

If you live in rental housing, you may also ask your landlord to install window locks. In a pinch, a sliding window frame can have a nail hammered into it that will prevent the window from being opened any further than desired. There are ways to jury-rig other window styles, and until a permanent fix can be implemented, don't hesitate to do what you need to do to prevent an escape.

The law provides for reasonable accommodation for disabilities. You can't demand remodeling that is frivolous, unreasonable, or abusive of the disability laws, but safety and security are reasonable expectations. Asking the landlord to fence the entire yard so your child can play outside is unreasonable; but if you live in a rental with inadequate locks or other safety concerns, the landlord must immediately address and correct these issues without penalty of eviction.

CHAPTER 5

Communication

Difficulty communicating is, without a doubt, the most serious impairment a person on the autism spectrum experiences. When a person—particularly a child—is unable to communicate, it is very difficult to understand and meet his needs. This can lead to a feeling of being unsafe and insecure.

The Nonverbal Person

Communicating with a nonverbal child intimidates many people. If a child understands language, even if he is unable to speak, it is hard enough to communicate, but if a child doesn't understand language, communication becomes much more difficult as well as emotionally trying.

 Alert

> It is important to find the best way to communicate with your child and stick to it. Each child is a unique human being and parents will soon find out what works best for their child. They are with their son or daughter twenty-four hours a day and can help the professionals decide on the best method of communication.

And You Thought It Was Baby Talk!

When parents bring home their newborn, they begin communicating nonverbally with cooing and nonsense sounds. These are the beginnings of communication. Humming tunes to a baby is another form of communication. It is through the tone and the rhythm of the voice that messages are sent. Although a baby does not have the ability to understand complex messages, he begins to learn about communication from the sounds and their cadence.

Parents learn as well how to understand nonverbal communication. They learn to recognize when their baby cries if it is a cry of hunger, discomfort, pain, or any number of things that are being communicated. Those cries, and the subsequent response by a parent, are forms of reciprocal communication.

If only communication stayed that simple. However, as a child matures, his needs include much more than just hunger or comfort. He needs to convey emotions, complex needs, and desires, and it is very difficult to do this without language. To keep things in perspective, remember that you have already established communication with your child. Yes, it was at a very young age and, yes, it isn't a fully efficient language. But you have the basics and you know more about nonverbal communication than you realize.

 Essential

Talking to a human being is different from talking to a pet. However, there are some valuable lessons here for the parent of a child with autism—body language, tone of voice, and visual cues all help to effectively communicate a message.

Trust Yourself and Pull Out the Stops

Much of the success in communication is about trust. If you believe your child will not understand, can never understand, and doesn't want to understand, you will probably find that to be true.

But if you believe he can understand much more than anyone realizes and you continue to communicate with that belief, you will find that his abilities will increase.

Never assume that your words and sentences are not understood. Your child's receptive language may not be at 100 percent, but something, somewhere, will get through and that is all you need to build on. Talk to your child as you would any child. Don't talk down to him, and don't talk over his head. Work at getting eye contact so he can see your facial expressions. Stand in front of him so he can see your body language, even if he appears to be totally oblivious of it. Consider your tone of voice and use every visual clue you can think of.

As the light begins to dawn for your child, and he realizes language is a useful tool, he will begin to attempt to understand it. It is a long and hard road for both parent and child, without a doubt. As the foundation begins with very little, and seemingly unimportant, understanding of minor words, you will realize that more complex receptive language skills can and will develop. Trust yourself.

Lacking Conceptual Images

For people with normal speech development, it is very difficult to communicate without using concepts. Things are big or bigger, happy or joyous, under, over . . . the list is endless. The human mind is built on and works through the understanding of concepts. But for someone with autism, concepts are very difficult. Can effective communication happen without relying on the conceptual imagery everyone uses each day?

A Language of Concept

Language by its very nature is conceptual. We believe, because we have been taught and have seen the result, that words are truly representative of something. If you go into an ice cream shop and ask for a large cone, you have certain expectations that you believe the other person understands. Generally, people do understand, and if they don't, they may ask for additional information.

Concepts within language are an obstacle for children with autism. When a word is first learned, whether verbal or through another form of communication, the use of that word has a hard and fast rule: a dog is always a dog; a cat is always a cat. But red? That is very subjective. Ask someone to buy you a red hat and you will learn how many shades of red there are. Concepts such as "quiet," "hungry," or "tired" are even harder to grasp. Only time and experience can teach these lessons. Speaking normally with your child and using visual clues will help the process along, but there is no definitive method to teach a concept.

Echolalia

As a child with autism begins to learn speech, it is common for her to repeat words without using those words for any communication or meaning. This is known as echolalia and, as stated earlier, it is one of the distinguishing factors of classical autism. For example, a parent might show a shirt to a child and ask, "Is this your shirt or your brother's?" The response may be "Brother's." This may not mean that your child has signed off on the property in question; she may simply be repeating the last word she heard. If you are in doubt, test by using the question again, but reversing the order of words. If she repeats a different word, you can be sure it is echolalia.

 Essential

When talking to your child, use universal signs to help her understand. Spread your arms to indicate "big." Mock shiver for "cold." Use clues for your child to help her link the word with the object or action. As linkages occur, language will begin to make sense and communication will be more effective.

Echolalia is frustrating to parents because they can see that the mechanics of language, such as the voice, are working fine, yet there is no spontaneous speech. The child may repeat words she has heard during the day or words that are common to her routine. "Everyone sit down," "it's lunchtime," or "here kitty, kitty" are examples of phrases that might be said with no meaning attached. When your child engages in echolalia in response to a question, try to guide her to the correct answer and gently correct her. If she is playing alone and you hear repeated phrases and words, ignore them. It is not helpful to try to stop a behavior that is harmless; she is unaware this is an inappropriate social behavior.

Receptive Speech

People who have normal speech abilities take the skill for granted. Speech is the exchange of ideas from one mind to another in a meaningful way. Receptive speech is the ability of the human mind to hear spoken language from another person and decipher it into a meaningful mental picture or thought pattern, which is understood and then used by the recipient. Speech is one of the things that separates humans from the animal world.

A Confusing World

When a person has a deficit in his receptive language skills, the entire world is a mystery. People with autism are often assumed to be like people with deafness. But the inability to relate to others shows the difference between the two conditions. People with deafness can't hear sound, but they can understand the language and all the conceptual images within the words and put those to use. People with autism hear the words but not the meaning behind them. They may understand a fair amount of communication in the framework of their own mental processes, or they may understand little. Either way, they are operating on a different wavelength.

During early intervention, you will have a good idea of how well your child's receptive speech is operating. Children who have learned the appropriate use of the words "mommy," "daddy," "hungry," and the like are beginning to understand that these words have a use. They are learning to understand how that usage applies to them. A child with receptive speech skills will understand "pick up your toys" and "don't touch that." If your child does not turn in response to hearing his own name, does not have the ability to name certain objects after seeing them, or disregards verbal commands—and a hearing problem has been ruled out—there is a receptive speech problem.

 Fact

Don't think your child with autism is ignoring what you say to him if he shows no reaction or withdraws into his own world. He is not deliberately tuning you out. He may just not understand the meaning of what you are saying and not know how to react.

Improving Understanding

A speech therapist will hopefully be working with your child if he lacks the ability to understand language. Other therapists should dovetail their therapy with the speech therapist's exercises so your child learns that language is useful. Children do not resist speech when they are autistic, as was commonly thought years ago. It is to their advantage to understand and use speech; but many just can't. It is as if there is a gap between the ears and the brain, almost as though a piece of electrical equipment has shorted out.

You, too, will probably be working with your child at home. In everything you and your family do, try to show your child that language is something in which he can participate. If your child is totally or essentially nonverbal, go slowly. Big picture books are helpful, as are flashcards. Avoid teaching conceptual words. If you try to explain "big" versus "small" with examples, your child may become confused. A big dog? Is the important word "dog" or "big"? Stick with nouns until your child starts to acquire receptive language skills and has a foundation to build on. Pronouns are also very difficult to understand when receptive speech skills are poor. Use people's names or speak in the third person to help comprehension.

 Essential

Pronouns are conceptual and should not be used unless a child has advanced speaking abilities. Speaking in the third person will be less confusing and frustrating. It is hard for a child with autism to understand that others have their own thoughts, and it's even more confusing when pronouns are used.

Expressive Speech

Expressive speech is the use of words and language verbally to communicate a concept or thought. If a person has expressive speech, they have some degree of receptive speech. Children learn their expressive speech by imitation. By hearing words from their parents, they learn how to use language as a tool. The first words a baby says are actually a sign that receptive speech has been working effectively for quite some time.

It is important for a child to be able to use speech, so if a child does not, there is a reason. Many parents will ask, "How do I encourage my child to talk without forcing her?" Encouraging a child to speak is good, but forcing her to talk may cause great stress and is not wise. There is a fine line between the two, but after some time this interaction will become second nature. Hold up a cookie or something your child loves to eat and say "cookie?" She will not repeat it right away, but eventually she will, if there is no hearing or other problem. When she does, give her the cookie and praise her. Some children respond well to applause; others do not like the noise. The phrase "good job" is soon recognized as praise. The important thing is not to withhold the cookie because she doesn't say the word. Remember, expressive and receptive speech are tied closely together, and safety and security are partly learned through communication. Continue meeting her needs and wants as if she were speaking, and your child will begin to see the usefulness of language.

Many experts state that if a child is not speaking by the age of six, she is unlikely to speak at all. However, this is not always true. Many parents will report that their child began speaking for no apparent reason at the age of puberty. Some children have startled their parents quite dramatically by being silent for over a decade and then suddenly communicating their first verbalization in a complete and appropriate sentence. Others will tentatively begin talking with a few words here and there before trying a phrase. It is possible that a child with autism will not speak at all, but don't give up. You may hear that voice yet.

Sign Language

Sign language is the preferred language for people who lack verbal communication ability. American Sign Language (ASL) is the third most commonly used language in the United States. Only English and Spanish are spoken more than sign language.

The beauty of sign language is that it is convenient, portable, doesn't require any special equipment, and is standard through-out the United States. The major disadvantage—and this is one that can and should be overcome—is that the language has to be learned by all family members, not just the child with autism.

American Sign Language

There are two major forms of sign language. The most widely used by the deaf community is ASL. ASL is a language that allows people with deafness to "hear" the same things the rest of the population can hear. Speeches, concerts, plays, and many other public events have an ASL interpreter present for translation. ASL is standardized and used consistently throughout the United States.

Many communities have sign language classes. If you decide to use sign language in your family, it is very helpful to take classes so you can teach your other children and your child with autism. There are also many books, videos, and computer programs that can help. These are very handy for parents and siblings of the child learning sign language.

Exact English

The other sign language, usually preferred by the autism community, is Exact English. Exact English is based on ASL but has some important differences that make this the preferred method. The learning curve is a little easier than ASL, but the difference is not significant. If you know ASL, you can work with Exact English very easily. Learning ASL will only make Exact English easier, so don't hesitate to get instruction on ASL. A book with the Exact English signs will show the differences and should be all the extra help, beyond learning ASL, that you might need.

 Fact

Check on the Internet for books on sign language. Some excellent books have large drawings of each sign and have signs arranged in alphabetical order. This is a quick way to reference a sign if you have forgotten it. It is also a good way to learn new signs.

The primary difference between Exact English and ASL is that ASL relies upon the use of conceptual thinking. Keeping in mind that sign language was developed for a community that had full receptive speech, the motions and gestures of ASL were created to say as much as possible quickly and economically. Entire phrases are often one single sign, and many of these phrases include words that are conceptual in nature. "I love you," for example, can be said three different ways: spelling out the letters of each of the three words (eight signs), signing one sign per word (three signs), or by using one sign that represents the entire phrase. ASL uses one sign for the entire phrase whereas Exact English uses one sign per word. This is helpful for children with autism as they learn about conceptual ideas.

Another advantage of Exact English is that it is accessible for the entire family. As a child learns a new sign, the parents can also learn the same sign. The alphabet can easily be learned by the entire family and can be used to spell out words—if a child understands words by reading. For these children, signing with Exact English helps brings words off the paper and into everyday usage.

It is very common for a child to learn a sign and then verbalize the word that the sign represents. However, this is not always the case, nor should it be the goal in teaching your child sign language. But, if this is the case with your child, speaking while signing will be an opportunity to develop more language skills. Your child may not be able to leave signing behind altogether, but as verbalization accompanies the signs, your child's skills in receptive communication will improve along with expressive speech.

Communication Boards

Many children on the autism spectrum who have limited or no verbal ability learn communication with a communication board. This is a form of augmentative and alternative communication (AAC).

Many styles of communication boards are helpful for a person with autism. The options range from complex, computer-run programs that are used to communicate, to systems as simple to use as a set of flashcards. There are systems you can purchase and systems you can make at home. Each child will have his own needs, and the most important issue is to personalize the board to meet those needs.

Picture Exchange Communication System (PECS)

The picture communication system (PCS) is the most widely used communication board for children and adults with autism. The beauty of this tool is that the learning curve is very low, and the system can be used immediately.

All that is necessary are photographs or drawings that represent people and things (nouns), actions (verbs), and concepts such as size and color (adjectives).

This system is favored because of its ease of use. One downside is that as a person's vocabulary grows, the collection can become unwieldy as more and more cards are added. However, there are some systems that organize cards into categories, which make utilization of many cards more practical. It can also be difficult for a child to learn concepts from cards; if a card has a blue circle, is he communicating the color or the shape? To find out more about this tool, check out the website of the Picture Exchange Commission at *www.pecs.com*.

Building a Communication Board

If you choose to use PECS, you can test it out very easily with your child. Take photographs, or cut pictures out of magazines, and have them laminated. Home laminating machines can also be purchased and will be handy to have around. Laminate about ten to fifteen cards, each one just a few inches square. Attach the cards together with a loose-leaf ring—these rings can be purchased separately—and show them to your child. As he learns that pointing to the picture of the television means he wishes to watch a program, the value of the cards will be learned. Make them relevant to your child's life so they are uniquely his own. Put them in a fanny pack and have him wear it so he has constant access to the cards.

 Essential

When you create a communication system, it's a good idea to make copies and records of your cards. If a card is lost or if you upgrade your system, you will want to keep the same pictures. Putting this on a computer will make your life easier; create a file with all of the pictures that are being used. Back it up on a CD or portable flash drive.

There are more sophisticated systems available that will open your child's world in a remarkable way. You are only limited by your own creativity and what you develop for your child's needs.

Other Communication Methods

One method of communication that is very reliable for individuals with autism is the keyboard. Many children who cannot speak are extremely efficient readers and writers. They may not be able to say they are thirsty and need a drink of water, but they are able to type it on a simple word-processing program. Even a simple text file on a desktop computer, a laptop, or handheld computer device will work. If your child seems to understand language and reads, try typing a simple question. "What is your name?" is a good one with which to start. She may look at you, unsure of what you want. Say the question while you point to the words on the screen and then point to the keyboard. If she understands how to communicate through writing, she will attempt to provide the answer. Coach her a bit as you begin. You will know very quickly whether this tool works for your child.

If you elect to use keyboard communication, consider a handheld computer device. They are portable and have word-processing programs that operate either with the device's small keyboard or with handwriting-recognition programs using a stylus. There is an added benefit of having a calendar on the small computer; most people with autism instinctively understand calendars and clocks and will use them to maintain their schedule and routine. It is also possible to play games on a handheld computer, which can be a great deal of fun and a good distraction for times when a child might be bored.

 Alert

A wise teacher or speech therapist will know there are many nonverbal methods of communication and will work hard to find whatever it takes to establish effective communication. However, if you feel the system being taught to your child is not the best one for her, talk with your child's teachers or request a consultation with an assistive technology consultant. This may have to be done by requesting a new IEP (Individual Education Program). Don't be afraid to challenge a system that doesn't seem to be working or is causing your child stress.

A very controversial communication tool is the method of facilitated communication (FC). This technique involves another person assisting a nonverbal person's efforts to communicate. The support may be as simple as providing encouragement to boost the self-confidence of someone who is unable to speak. It can also involve steadying or guiding a hand to pictures or words if necessary. People with tremors, nerve damage, or poor muscle control may require some physical assistance. The point of contention with FC is the question of whether a facilitator influences what is being communicated. Opinions vary widely and parents who are considering this form of communication would be wise to research it thoroughly to reassure themselves about their choice.

The most important thing any parent, caretaker, family member, teacher, or professional can remember about communication is that there is no one right way that works for every child. A child with autism is just like any other child: each is unique and will respond to different styles of learning and working. If one child works well with keyboard communication and another can't figure it out, but is a whiz with PECS, it doesn't mean one child is more advanced than the other. It simply means they are two distinct personalities.

Additional Social Strategies

Role-playing can be very helpful in developing social skills. Because so many kids with autism want to stay by themselves or just do things on their computers, it is important to get them involved with the world outside themselves.

One way to help broaden your child's world is to have him practice different social situations, using storybooks or pictures to model behavior. Often siblings can get a child with autism to play or become involved with a game or project. The most important thing is not to push your child to the point that he becomes anxious and withdraws even further. Every child will have his own timetable about allowing others to come close.

CHAPTER 6

Meltdowns and Discipline

Perhaps the true initiation of parenting a child with autism is the baptism by fire of a meltdown. Once just a scientific term in nuclear physics, the autism community has adopted the word. Seeing and experiencing a meltdown makes it clear why only this term applies. Dealing with meltdowns is a bit like dealing with a tornado: You have very little warning, and all you can do is ride it out.

Discipline

Children must be guided into the proper way to behave. Discipline does not need to be an angry or negative experience. If handled properly, it can be positive and motivating for everyone. Important things to keep in mind include:

- Positive reinforcement is much more effective than negative.
- Make the discipline fit the severity of the unacceptable behavior.
- Parents must be in agreement on what behaviors are to be disciplined and what is to be overlooked.
- Each parent should share in disciplining; it should not be the exclusive burden of one parent.

- Parents must have a policy on spanking, recognizing that to a child with autism it is violence. If spanking is used, it should only be when the child, another person, or pet is at risk of being harmed. Verbal and physical abuse is not an option. Ever.
- It is a good idea for parents to have a talk about how they feel about discipline. If a child throws a tantrum or has a meltdown and these decisions have not been made, it can be difficult to know how to handle it. The middle of your child's meltdown is not the best time to discuss child-rearing philosophies.

Autistic Meltdowns Versus Temper Tantrums

If you need to explain a meltdown to someone who doesn't have a child with autism, just define it as a bad temper tantrum, and let the topic go. It is unlikely that the finer points of a meltdown will be understood. But, if you mention the word to parents who have children with autism, you will get knowing and sympathetic looks. Rest assured, your child is not the only one who has these rather unique behavioral episodes.

Temper Tantrums

A temper tantrum is usually straightforward. A child does not get his or her own way and, as grandma would say, "pitches a fit." This is not to discount the temper tantrum. They are not fun for anyone.

Tantrums have several qualities that distinguish them from meltdowns:

- A child having a tantrum will look occasionally to see if her behavior is getting a reaction.

- A child in the middle of a tantrum will take precautions to be sure she won't get hurt.
- A child who throws a tantrum will attempt to use the social situation to her benefit.
- When the situation is resolved, the tantrum will end as suddenly as it began.
- A tantrum will give you the feeling that the child is in control, although she would like you to think she is not.
- A tantrum is thrown to achieve a specific goal and once the goal is met, things return to normal.

 Fact

> If you feel like you are being manipulated by a tantrum, you are right. A tantrum is nothing more than a power play by a person not mature enough to play a subtle game of internal politics. Hold your ground and remember who is in charge.

A temper tantrum in a child who does not have autism is relatively easy to handle. Parents need to simply ignore the behavior and refuse to give the child what she is demanding. Tantrums usually result when a child makes a request to have or do something that the parent denies. Upon hearing the parent's "no," the child uses the tantrum as a last-ditch effort to get her way.

The qualities of a temper tantrum vary from child to child. When children decide this is the way they are going to handle a given situation, each child's style will dictate how the tantrum plays out. Some children will throw themselves on the floor, screaming and kicking. Others will hold their breath, thinking that this "threat" on their life will cause parents to bend. Some children will be extremely vocal and repeatedly yell, "I hate you," for the world to hear. A few children will attempt bribery or blackmail, and although these are quieter methods, this is just as much of a tantrum as screaming. Of course, there are the very few children who pull out all the stops and use all these methods.

Effective parenting, whether a child has autism or not, is learning that you are in control, not the child. This is not a popularity contest. You are not there to wait on your child and indulge her every whim. Buying her every toy she wants isn't going to make her any happier than if you say no. There is no easy way out of this parenting experience. Sometimes you just have to dig in and let the tantrum happen.

 Fact

> Ignoring a child having a temper tantrum will help the tantrum to stop. A child wants attention and also wants to get her own way. Some children scream until they get the desired result. Kids are very smart and know exactly which of an adult's buttons to press.

Meltdowns

If the tantrum is straightforward, the meltdown is every known form of manipulation, anger, and loss of control that a child can muster. The problem is that the loss of control soon overtakes the child. She needs you to recognize this behavior and rein her in, as she is unable to do so. A child with autism in the middle of a meltdown desperately needs help to gain control. Distinct qualities of a meltdown include:

- During a meltdown, a child with autism does not look, nor care, if those around her are reacting to her behavior.
- A child in the middle of a meltdown does not consider her own safety.
- A child in a meltdown has no interest or involvement in the social situation.

- Meltdowns will usually continue as though they are moving under their own power and wind down slowly.
- A meltdown conveys the feeling that no one is in control.
- A meltdown usually occurs because a specific want has been denied and after that point has been reached, nothing can satisfy the child until the situation is over.

Unlike tantrums, meltdowns can leave even experienced parents at their wit's end, unsure of what to do. When you think of a tantrum, the classic image of a child lying on the floor with kicking feet, swinging arms, and a lot of screaming is probably what comes to mind. This is not even close to a meltdown. A meltdown is best defined by saying it is a total loss of behavioral control. It is loud, risky at times, frustrating, and exhausting.

Meltdowns may be preceded by "silent seizures." This is not always the case, so don't panic, but observe your child after she begins experiencing a meltdown. Does the meltdown have a brief period before onset where your child "spaces out"? Does she seem like she had a few minutes of time when she was totally uninvolved with her environment? If you notice this trend, speak to your pediatric neurologist. This may be the only manifestation of a seizure that you will be aware of.

 Essential

If your child launches into a meltdown, remove her from an area where she could be injured or that she might damage. Glass shelving and doors may become the target of an angry foot, and avoiding injury to your child or others as well as surrounding objects is the top priority during a meltdown.

Another cause of a meltdown can be a health issue such as migraines. A child who suffers from migraines may be at greater risk for a meltdown because the migraine acts as a trigger. A migraine may come on suddenly and the pain is so debilitating, a child's behavior may spiral quickly downward resulting in a meltdown. Watch for telltale signs such as sensitivity to light, head holding, or unusual sensitivity to sound.

Handling a Meltdown in Public

Any parent who is raising a child with autism will tell you that meltdowns are more common in public locations. Stores, malls, fairs—anywhere there are a lot of people, activity, and noise raises the odds of a meltdown. It is common enough that many parents will do anything they can to avoid being in those environments with their child.

To Market, To Market

Inevitably, your child will experience a meltdown in a large, brightly lit variety store. Every parent knows about these stores—the one-stop shopping that turns into an ordeal and fiasco. A parent related the following story about her son, and any parent of a child with autism will laugh and cry at the same time; they all know what this is like.

"We went in for groceries and various items. It was a big shopping trip and I couldn't find a babysitter that day. I also couldn't put it off any longer. We did okay until we went by the home gardening section. A big, and I mean very big, lawn sprinkler was on display—a sprinkler that was a dead ringer for the tractor that my little boy loves, all bright green and yellow and just about the right size for him to sit on. At first he quietly asked 'tractor,' or, should I say, demanded it. I could see the look. I knew he had decided the "tractor" was coming home with us. And I knew it wasn't. The volume of his voice went higher and

higher until you could hear the word tractor being screeched all over the store! We made our way to the checkout line, but by then, he was in complete meltdown. I am sure everyone thought I was the meanest mom in the world for not buying my little boy a toy tractor. The meltdown continued into the parking lot and into the car; he was sweating, crying, screaming, and attempting to hit anything or anyone he could. He totally lost it. I was exhausted and so was he." She added, *"I now make an extra effort to find a babysitter and have my radar up to scope out the aisles around us to avoid any more tractors."*

 Fact

If your child begins a meltdown by putting his hands over his ears or eyes, you can be sure he is experiencing sensory overload. He might even cover your mouth with his hand to prevent another sound. The best thing is to move him to a low-sensory environment; a dark, quiet, and cool place will help.

This mom handled a difficult situation well. She had shopping that had to be done; this wasn't an optional trip to the store. And once the meltdown was in full swing, she was almost done. It wouldn't have been convenient for her to leave the store and return later to redo an enormous shopping. She kept her cool, didn't give in, and didn't worry about the opinions of others while her son spun totally out of control.

The Rudeness of Others

The little boy with, or in this case without, the tractor had a real advantage that day. His mother was not threatened or concerned about the opinions of others. It has been said that parents of kids with special needs have to develop thicker skins, and it must be true. But regardless of how thick-skinned you are, an insult to your child cuts, and cuts deeply.

For some reason, in public, many people feel it is their duty to point out all of the mistakes they believe you are making in raising your child. This is even more common if your child is mentally challenged or if the child "expert" has no children. Just remember: You can't change the world; you can only change your little corner of it. How your child feels and how you affect his life are far more important.

Keep in mind that some people are receptive to learning and you may have a chance to educate someone about autism. There are also subtle clues you can use to notify people without saying a word that you have a child with special needs. An example would be signing to your child.

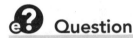 **Question**

Someone called my child a cruel name. Best advice?
If the person called your child a goat, it wouldn't make him one. However, it is hurtful and shows a lack of knowledge and sensitivity. A simple explanation is wise if you feel the individual is receptive. Otherwise, ignore it. The person can move on to be unpleasant somewhere else.

It is very common for people in public places such as the store in the tractor incident to stare and make comments very critical of a child in the middle of a meltdown. People will say things about your lack of control over your child or direct unflattering comments toward your child, and as much as you would like to throttle them or talk back, resist the urge. Excuse your child's behavior politely with the brief explanation of "he is disabled," and drop it. If a person persists in making comments and it is clear he is not interested in educating himself, move yourself and your child to another location. If, on the other hand, it is a staff member who is making snide comments at the place you are visiting, ask to speak with a manager. The supervisor needs to know that the staff member does not understand the problems of a child with a disability and steps should be taken to educate the individual.

Defusing a Meltdown

Although it sounds like a cliché, the best way to handle a meltdown in progress is to defuse it. Sometimes that is much easier said than done, but it comes down to one simple perspective: Choose your battles. How you choose them will depend on your personality and your child's personality.

When Your Child Understands

When a child understands and manipulates a meltdown to get her own way, you are dealing with an intelligent child who can stop the behavior if it is caught in time. Keep in mind that a child with autism, regardless of how well she understands a meltdown is unacceptable, will not be able to control it once a certain point is reached. The goal is to try to prevent a child that is cognizant of her behavior from reaching that point. Steps you can take include:

1. Recognize the signs of an impending meltdown.
2. Determine if there is a certain trigger before the meltdown and what it is.
3. If the trigger is fairly insignificant, such as your child wanting to hold a red ball in the store, decide if it is worth it. A red ball is a small price to pay for a quiet shopping trip.
4. If the trigger is something that is not possible to resolve, such as the one in the tractor story, try to distract your child by moving to another location and find a substitute to divert her attention.
5. If you are in a restaurant and a meltdown is approaching, reach for a new or very special toy you have hidden in

your purse. Something complex, like a handheld puzzle, can work well.

6. As you are working to distract your child, speak softly to her about her behavior and let her know that it needs to stop. Don't dwell on what she can't have at that moment, but reiterate that she needs to slow down and stay in control. Stay calm so she has no idea you are panicking over the thought that she might lose it.

7. Persist in any calming techniques that work for your child. Some children will respond to a hug while others will not want to be touched; this is a matter of "whatever works."

You will not always be able to defuse a child bent on having a meltdown. If the cycle progresses and he reaches the point-of-no-return, you have two options: You can decide to ride it out or you can leave the environment.

Much of riding it out depends on where you are. Right in the middle of a wedding may not be the best time to try to work with behavior modification. It would be best not to take a child prone to meltdowns to a special occasion such as a wedding. Other people do have the right to an undisturbed environment. However, in the real world, the everyday world, your child has to learn to operate in society, and society will hopefully learn to deal with children who have autism. However, it is more prudent to leave an area if others are being disturbed unfairly or if you feel the situation could become dangerous.

When Your Child Does Not Understand

A child who does not understand what type of behavior is wanted or expected is more challenging to deal with when a meltdown is about to occur. It is important to remain calm because your child is already on a sensory overload and if you are upset, you will aggravate the situation. Keep your voice even, quiet, and calm no matter what happens.

The primary tool a parent has with a child in a meltdown is distraction. It is useless to try to reason with a child who does not understand that her actions are not acceptable. Molding a child's behavior through distraction and positive reinforcement will be a much more effective tool and hopefully prevent future meltdowns as well.

Distraction is 50 percent preparation and 50 percent creativity. Preparation is the easy part. Mom or dad can put items to distract their child in a backpack or tote bag to have when a meltdown begins. When it becomes apparent that the explosion is about to begin, being able to pull "the rabbit out of the hat" is your best bet. Comforting toys, such as a favorite stuffed animal, are wise choices, as are toys that are so fascinating they just can't be ignored.

 Question

Will I know if the distraction has things under control?
Your child will either become engrossed in the distraction toy and the meltdown will fade away or he will use the distraction as part of the meltdown. If your child throws the "distraction" toy back at you, it is a sign you need to get creative.

Creativity is a bit more challenging. Think of toys your child enjoys and finds pleasure in. Every child is different; there is no "stop-the-meltdown-toy" available. Use the knowledge you have of your child and let his reactions guide you as you consider helpful distractions.

Behavior Modification

What is easier than handling a meltdown or defusing one? Avoiding it altogether. You may feel right now that you have little control over your child's tantrums and meltdowns, and this may be true.

However, there are things you can do to minimize the frequency and severity of the outbursts.

Working with a child's behavior is always the first step a parent should take. If you can modify his undesirable behavior, your child will be happier and those around him will be as well. Don't ever think you are being cruel by working to alter unacceptable behaviors. You will be met with resistance; no one likes to change, least of all a child with autism. But at times, change is necessary, and when a child has a predilection to tantrums, his behavior must be modified.

Applied Behavioral Analysis (ABA)

ABA is one of the most widely used methods of treating children with autism. Dr. Ivar Lovaas, the founder of the Lovaas Institute, is the creator of ABA. His goal in working with children with autism has been to modify behaviors that are inappropriate and replace them with appropriate behaviors. His website is *www .lovaas.com.*

As Dr. Lovaas developed his theories of behavior, the foundation of his work centered on how people treated one another and whether it was environment or genetics that caused people to act a certain way. By a twist of fate, he began working with children with autism and observed that modifying behaviors was not that difficult. The hard part was keeping those behaviors solidly in place after the behavior had been successfully changed.

Dr. Lovaas realized that the main difference in behaviors between children with autism and those without could be found in their learning styles. Children who do not have autism are constantly learning. Even beyond school, every moment of every day is a learning experience for a child; learning is a constant and dynamic process. However, a child with autism goes to school and learns for a prescribed number of hours each day. When he returns home, the structured learning is over for the day and he retreats into his own world.

Continuing ABA Therapy

The key to modifying behavioral problems in a child with autism suddenly became obvious to Dr. Lovaas. A child could not come to the Institute, work on ABA, and then just return home after successful therapy was completed; the newly acquired behaviors broke down and everyone was back to square one. It may seem obvious now, but at the time, this was quite a breakthrough. Parents were taught how to continue the ABA therapy at home and changes in their child's behaviors became permanent.

If behavioral issues have had a profound impact on your child's life, and consequently your family's life, you may want to investigate behavior modification. See Appendix B for resources to learn more about this technique. Meltdowns and tantrums, if your child is inclined to them, will not disappear entirely, but with training and therapy, there is an excellent chance the number and severity of these outbursts can be reduced dramatically.

Neurofeedback

This is a relatively new treatment for higher functioning children with autism although it has been used in the past for other disorders. The idea behind the therapy is that patients can be taught how to change their brain waves, which could then help to control anxieties, moods, and behavior. It is a time consuming and expensive treatment, and not covered by all health insurance plans, so it should not be undertaken without considerable thought and research.

A child undergoing neurofeedback has a special wire or electrode placed on her scalp as well as one on each ear. She is then placed in front of a computer, and a video-like game displays her brain waves. A therapist then shows parent and child how the child's thought patterns can change the brain waves. The child receives points when her brain waves are altered in certain ways. Initially, the therapist will want to see the child several times a week, but then the sessions revert to just once a week. This is a major time commitment for a parent and child.

Medications

When a child with autism is young and his behavior is unpredictable, it is miserable for him as well as everyone around him. Children with autism will often lash out physically, kicking, hitting, and/or biting, when they become angry. And, unfortunately, anger seems to be an emotion they readily display. If your child lashes out, take heart; you are not alone. It is a common behavior seen in children with autism.

There are several medications used to help in the control of unpredictable behaviors that children with autism will display. Parents are often reluctant to use it, but there are times when medication is appropriate and necessary. It is vital to remember that an out-of-control child is not a happy child, but a child who needs help. You have not failed as a parent if you and your physician decide medications are appropriate for your child.

 Alert

One medication used for aggression is risperidone. This is currently approved only for patients over age eighteen. If your teenager is on this medication watch for excessive weight gain and facial tics. If either of these occurs, visit your teen's physician to decide if the dosage needs to be adjusted.

If medications are prescribed for your child, and you are concerned about side effects or long-term use, talk to a pharmacist about your concerns. A pharmacist is one of the best resources for a discussion of these issues as well as for advice on medications, interactions between medicines, and which over-the-counter medications are safe for your child to use. In a support group meeting, ask other parents what medications they have used and how they feel about them; a support group can be very helpful as a medication becomes part of the routine. However, remember that these medicines are very potent, so if you have serious concerns or questions, it would be wise to seek professional advice.

CHAPTER 7

ASD and Effects on the Parents' Marriage

It is estimated that 50 to 75 percent of marriages fail in families with a disabled child. Exact statistics vary widely depending on the source, but the numbers are always high. It is a fact: Having a child with autism is hard on a marriage and a family. It is difficult for a couple, particularly when they are young, to remain a couple and have a child who is so far from what they had anticipated. Other people including doctors, therapists, teachers, and social workers become so much part of your life, that it feels they have become part of your marriage. It is hard to remember that you are still the same two people who fell in love, married, and planned to live happily ever after.

How Mom Is Affected

Pregnancy is an exciting time for a woman. The growing infant within her—as it begins to move and kick and then show a silhouette on an ultrasound—is the person she most anticipates meeting. It doesn't matter if it is a first child or the second or the tenth. This baby is often the focus of her thoughts.

When the baby is born and the doctor announces whether it is a boy or girl, invariably the first question heard is, "Is everything alright?" And what a relief it is when all ten fingers and toes are present and there are no disabilities. A healthy child has come into the world.

A Child Regressing

It is a shock to parents when they see their child's developmental progress begin to slip away slowly. Their beautiful baby, now approaching the toddler stage, with his few words and joyful reactions to the world around him, is changing. The words are fewer and fewer until they are heard no more. The interactive baby, who chuckled and had sparkling eyes just looking at mom and dad, now seems enclosed in a world of darkness where no one else can go.

Their child will no longer look at them, no longer tries to learn new words or even use those already learned, and doesn't seem to hear them. They will likely ask each other: "What have we done wrong?"

The Five Stages

There are usually five stages in a person's life. But the stages are different when your child has autism:

- **Infancy**—Mom's hopes, dreams, and visions of a new life are shattered with the realization that something has gone wrong.
- **Toddler years**—The child's mother begins to realize that the problems are not going away and must be coped with.
- **Young school age**—More dreams are lost as a child enters school and mom can see the contrast between her child and other children.
- **Older school age**—The child makes progress, but new concerns develop over challenges brought by puberty, adolescence, and the beginning of young adulthood.
- **Adulthood**—As the child becomes an adult, mom and dad become aware that they, too, are aging and they begin to

worry what will happen to their child when they are no longer able to provide care.

This is a lot for young parents to absorb. And parents often think through all five stages within a few months of the diagnosis. Considering most children are diagnosed with autism before they are two, a mom and dad live an entire child's lifetime around the time two candles are on a birthday cake. Stress, fear, denial, anxiety, confusion, anger, depression, and sadness are inevitable. It may be one of the hardest times in their lives.

Diagnosis and Adjustment

Mothers are deeply affected when professionals begin the process of diagnosing their child. The protective and maternal instincts within a mother are natural, so she is likely to resent all the "experts" who have suddenly intruded into the middle of her family's life.

 Essential

Mothers may feel frustrated when the experts can't give an immediate diagnosis. The testing for autism and other related conditions can take quite some time, and frustration with medical and other professionals is normal. The acceptance or adjustment to the diagnosis that will eventually come is at this point a long time off, and it is a tumultuous time.

Eventually all of the emotions that run amok within the mother will settle down, and although none of them ever disappear entirely, they generally become manageable and a sense of acceptance occurs. Mom will hopefully begin to adjust to the situation and start to reset goals and plans, accommodating the child's needs and abilities within that framework. There will always be times when she will feel sad or depressed; she will have spikes of anger at the situation when a problem arises that isn't easily solved, but she will have learned to accept or adjust and do what moms do best: love her child.

How Dad Is Affected

Dads are also affected by the realization that their child has been diagnosed on the autism spectrum, but the reactions of a father can be different from those of a mother. Men usually want to fix the problem quickly and when they learn they can't, they must reach an understanding that they have not failed. It is not their fault the child has autism any more than it is the mother's fault. Just like mothers, fathers progress through stages of understanding as their child with autism goes through life stages:

- **Infancy**—When a dad has a new infant, his pride and delight are unparalleled. When something goes wrong, it is hard for many fathers to come to terms with the disability, and they may take a long time to accept it. Usually a father grapples with acceptance of his child's autism longer than a mother.
- **Toddler years**—Realization begins to force its way into a father's mind. Fathers will either react with acceptance of the situation and begin to find ways to cope with it, or they will deny that it exists or look to blame someone. Denial is a common reaction for men, as well as many women, because they feel responsible for the events that occur within their family.
- **Young school age**—As a child enters school, fathers begin to see the deficits and often have trouble seeing the child's progress. It is important for therapists, physicians, and the child's mother to point out the progress being made so that the father can see the glass as half full. This stage is normal, and it will pass. Many dads feel responsible and frustrated that they can't fix the problem.

- **Older school age**—This is a time where fathers really shine if they have come to acceptance, which many have by this stage. The progress is evident and now the issues are ones that men can handle more comfortably. They must meet specific challenges and problem solving is the needed skill. Dad may find his problem-solving skills to be very useful and he will feel less like a failure and more like a dad.
- **Adulthood**—Like mom, dad becomes aware that his child has become an adult and that he will not always be there to protect his child. By this time, he and mom will hopefully have started estate and financial planning to protect their child, and worked on solving the issues that will face their child after they are gone.

Learning to Cope

Dad has a lot to absorb, just as Mom does. Men have different coping mechanisms from women, so they will process and absorb all of this differently. It is important for Mom to remember that Dad's method of dealing with the diagnosis of their child is no less valid than her own. It may seem that a man isn't handling the situation well, and perhaps there is some denial involved, but given time the acceptance or adjustment to the diagnosis will hopefully occur.

 Alert

A strong family is the key. For a father, it is vital to maintain strong bonds with your spouse and all your children. Fathers should try to help provide the needed emotional and spiritual leadership, so his wife or partner and other family members do not carry too great a burden.

It is hard for parents to adapt to the loss of the dreams they had for their child, and there will be a period of adjustment as Mom and Dad establish new goals. Women can do a lot to help their husbands adjust by understanding the psychology of wanting to "make it okay" that is often inherent to a male's nature.

Eventually, both parents will accept or adjust to the problem, and establish a routine. As these processes are happening, both Mom and Dad need to remember that their marriage is the first priority. Taking care of each other will enable them to take care of the rest of their family, and that includes their child with autism.

Keeping ASD from Affecting the Marriage

The strongest piece of advice most therapists will give a couple who has a child with autism is: "Do not allow autism to become your entire life." It is so easy to eat, breathe, and sleep autism, but it will do no good—for you, for your spouse, and not even for your child. There is enough stress within a marriage, and adding autism to the mix only ratchets up the stress level.

And stress in a marriage can result in short tempers, communication difficulties, allowing your life as a couple to fade away, and the worst possible situation, turning to others rather than each other for companionship and support. Turning away from the marriage is not the solution.

 Question

Autism has come between us. Now what do I do?
When you speak with your spouse or partner it would be best not to use the words "you never" or "you always." Your partner may not realize there are any problems, so start the conversation with "I feel." Good communication should help solve the problem. If not, some counseling would be a good idea.

Although your child has autism or another disorder on the spectrum, if you allow autism to take over your life, you will become socially isolated. Turn to each other for support and go to events, support groups, and other activities as a couple to strengthen your bond. You can become stronger because of autism and not allow it to unravel your marriage. It just takes time, effort, and a lot of love.

Maintaining and Creating Intimacy

One of the most difficult things in a marriage, let alone a marriage with a disabled child, is maintaining the intimacy unique to marriage. When a couple goes from being a man and a woman to being a mom and a dad, they often find it hard to remember they are still a man and a woman! The special intimacy that you knew before you had a child is just as important, perhaps even more important, than it was before. Sexuality is not the most important thing in a marriage, but it is the glue that holds marriage together and it is also important to remember that intimacy is not always about sex. So how do you keep intimacy alive when you have children, and especially a child with special needs? Here are just a few ideas for special moments:

- Go out on a date with each other. Schedule an actual date, go out, and talk about anything but autism.
- Celebrate every occasion you can think of: anniversaries of the first date, first kiss, first anything—just celebrate!
- Splurge on gifts for each other. You don't have to have a reason other than the fact that you love each other.
- Buy books on intimacy and sexuality. Have grandma watch the kids and go to a hotel for an evening. Enjoy each other as if it were the first time.
- Give each other massages with no sexuality expected. Just make the other person relax and feel good.
- Plan a picnic and lie on the ground looking at the clouds. Tell each other what you see in the clouds.

Remember, you are still the same woman and the same man who fell in love and got married. ASD has not changed that.

It isn't that hard to keep the spark alive or to relight it, if the years have allowed the flame to go out. Remember that the child who has brought some extra challenges and, yes, some stress as well, into your lives is a product of the love you have for each other. This child can only benefit from the closeness that you as a couple will have by the efforts you make to keep your intimate life alive.

Making Your Spouse a Priority

One of the most important priorities in your life is your spouse. People, and especially mothers, tend to let this priority slip from its proper placement, putting their children above their marriage. Although it sounds noble not to put anything above your children, in reality it is harmful for everyone, including the children. If anything is more important to you than your marriage, your marriage is at risk of failing. It is the foundation of the family.

 Alert

> One of the best things you can do for yourself, for your marriage, and for your children is to take a few minutes each day to meditate, or have a quiet time. It will rebalance and refresh your spirit. Everything will seem easier to manage.

Many people would feel guilty putting another adult, even a spouse, above their children. However, it is not a matter of viewing one person as more important than another. It is an understanding of how we need to attend to the obligations and responsibilities of our lives. A child cannot feel secure and grow up to the best of his ability if the family's foundation is insecure.

If a child's parents love each other and work hard to create the best relationship they possibly can, their child will feel that security within his own life. It has been said that there is no greater gift a father can give his children than to love their mother. It is also true that a mother can show nothing greater to her children than love for their father.

Children as a Priority

Most parents have no difficulty with this one! Children quickly, almost automatically, become the lights of our lives. Regardless if they have autism or not, these children are still the hope of our future. Children are the gift that brings joy, happiness, frustration, irritation, laughter, tears, and every possible emotion right into the center of our lives.

Many times, it is hard for some parents to remember that their children are more important than their work. Careers are a lifelong project, and a person with an occupation doesn't always understand that a child's needs are more critical than a deadline at the office. It is so easy to be caught up in the mentality that "it has to be done right now." In reality, the only jobs that have to be done "right now" are those of trauma surgeons and the like. So, if you are a physician, paramedic, firefighter, or have a career where peoples' lives are on the line, you may have to make some extra efforts to keep your job in its proper perspective without ignoring the needs of family members who depend on you.

For the majority of people, most career obligations can fit into a normal workday. There will hopefully be only a few career-related things that will keep you from your child's soccer games, concerts, or other activities that are part of the growing-up process. There will be many activities that your child with autism can participate in, and it is important for you to be there if possible.

Yes, there will be times you can't attend an activity or be at a doctor's appointment without risking your job, and in those situations all you can do is your best. Ask yourself if what you are doing at work is truly something you can't leave or if it is a self-imposed deadline. If it is something you are putting on yourself, take some time to analyze your priorities.

Valuing Extended Family

If you're like most people, you are part of a larger family unit; there are grandparents, in-laws, cousins, and other people who are part of your life. Those family members are important to you, your spouse, and your child. Growing up within an extended family is a wonderful privilege and provides another layer to a secure foundation for children. Extended family can be there to help you, just as you help them, and be part of very special relationships and memories.

However, it is important not to let the extended family relationships take over your life. This is where your priority system can actively come into play and assist in how you conduct your life. In any family, there are social occasions to attend: parties, showers, weddings, and other celebrations are part of the family experience. Most of these are good for the family and good for children, but they don't need to dictate your family's schedule.

 Essential

Many times during the year, particularly during the religious holidays, families find themselves going in fifty directions to do everything they want as well as everything that is expected of them. This year create a quieter holiday, and see if the sensory overload on your child is lessened.

Pacing your family's schedule is important. If your child is easily over-stimulated by too much activity, choose family occasions that are the least stressful for your child. If you are involved in social activities two or three times a week, you and your child may become too exhausted to attend to basic family needs. Saying "no" occasionally to various get-togethers is sometimes the best decision. Explain the situation to your extended family so they can still be involved with your child and learn as much about autism as possible.

Involve grandparents in the life of your child with autism if they are willing. This can be a difficult and touchy relationship at times, but understanding a few things about how grandparents may be thinking can save many hurt feelings. (More will be explained on this subject in Chapter 10.) Families have been created from love and, although we can't choose our families, we can choose how to interact with them.

Handling Your Work

If you already have a career established when you learn that your child has autism, it would be wise to schedule a meeting with your immediate supervisor and explain the situation. Have with you a few printouts about autism that you can leave with your boss if he or she is unfamiliar with the condition. A scientific journal isn't what you need, just some basic facts about autism. Remember, knowledge is power, and your supervisor's understanding about the various problems will help prevent misunderstandings in the future should you require time away from work due to your child's various doctor, therapy, or school appointments.

When you explain to your employer that your child has autism, emphasize that this should not affect your work performance. Keep in mind that your employer is there to run a business with the priority to make that business function as efficiently as possible. Volunteer to make up any missed time if this is a possibility.

If you work for a large company, ask if there is a way that your company can become involved with autism awareness causes.

Many companies will rally behind an employee who has a child on the autism spectrum and donate money to various fundraising campaigns.

 Fact

Many doctors and other professionals have at least one evening a week that they see patients. Try to find therapists and physicians who are available during evening hours to help relieve some of the stress of scheduling appointments. If you don't know of a doctor with convenient hours, ask at a support-group meeting.

Friends, Hobbies, and Everything Else

Life can be good. It is overwhelming at times, particularly when you have just learned your child has autism. But it can be good and full. Never allow yourself to think that because autism is now part of your life that you will no longer be able to enjoy all of the people and interests you have had over the years. You have a child with autism—the world has not ended.

Friends are a link to sanity. Meeting with them on a regular basis helps to maintain our mental health. It reminds us there is a world out there, and conversations beyond how to take care of children are a welcome escape. Be careful, though, that you don't rely on friends more than a spouse, or spend so much time with friends that other parts of your life are neglected. Visit with friends and make plans to do things that have nothing to do with autism, but keep those relationships in their proper perspective.

Hobbies, sports, and activities of any kind promote health and well-being, both mentally and physically. If you enjoyed certain hobbies or travel before, try to continue these pursuits, at least on a limited basis. Yes, you will have to make adjustments, but as long as you keep things in the proper perspective, you should be able to do many of the things that are important to you and your family. You will hopefully with time learn the skills to integrate autism into your life. Your experience will grow and you will become more confident in your understanding of ASD.

CHAPTER 8

The Single Parent and the ASD Child

O ne of the most difficult roles a parent will ever assume is that of the single parent. It doesn't matter how a parent arrived at that state: divorced, widowed, or single by choice, it is a daily challenge. When a mom or dad is a single parent and there is a child with autism to care for, the challenges can make life feel like a true burden. But it can be done. It just takes a little more effort, organization, and, of course, a lot of love.

Unique Challenges

Although parenting always has challenges, single parenting can be extremely stressful, as well as rewarding. Knowing solutions can be found to most problems is the first step toward keeping you from feeling overwhelmed. Almost every problem has a solution. Many of the solutions you will need are related to work, which will be addressed in the next section. Other challenges are about you—the single mom or dad. The real trick to success as a parent, whether single or married, is not losing yourself in the parenting process. There are some issues of which every single parent needs to be aware. Working on the solutions before they become problems can greatly reduce your stress.

The Difficulty of a Social Life

Everyone needs social interaction, and a single parent of a child with autism is no exception. In addition to caring for your child with autism, you may be working full time, meeting the needs of your other children, and taking care of the home—leaving you little free time. You may have other obligations, too, such as school or community activities. Exhaustion takes on a new meaning, and social life is so far on the back shelf it is hard to remember what it was like to have one.

Even so, it is important to carve out time in your schedule for social activities. This can be whatever activity you enjoy—hiking, biking, dancing, card games, movies, eating out . . . whatever you like doing with other people. The key is interaction with friends. Adults who do not spend time with friends begin to resent their schedule, their lives, and possibly their children. It is normal to feel that way and the best way to avoid the problem is to schedule time to socialize.

No Partner to Commiserate with Daily

One major advantage that married parents have is companionship. Yes, there are many other advantages as well, but nothing is quite like being with a person who knows and understands the daily problems you encounter. Having someone with whom you can pour out your frustrations and victories of the day is a relief. It is human nature to want to share.

If you don't have anyone in your life with whom you can share on a daily basis, work at developing friendships that are true give-and-take relationships. A local support group that includes single parents might be helpful. Some support groups have a network of parents who are on "phone duty" that you can call at any time when you need to talk or vent your emotions.

Potential Difficulties with Ex-Spouse and In-Laws

If you are single by divorce or made the choice not to marry your child's other parent, hopefully you have been able to create a good working relationship for the benefit of the child. If not, and the sparks fly very time you see each other. it would be wise to consult a counselor. Even if your marriage has no chance in the world, there needs to be a peaceful environment for the child.

 Essential

> Often in the case of separated parents, the child will show behavioral problems when visiting the noncustodial parent. Questions about the ability of either parent to care for the child arise, when really the change in routine is to blame.

Children with autism may seem to be unaware of the environment around them, but they usually are much more in tune with the emotions of others than it appears. If the parents are arguing or fighting, the child is apt to act out with aggressive and belligerent behaviors. The adults in the situation, by keeping their own tempers, can prevent this. Remember that although your relationship may be over, the relationship both of you have with your child is not, nor hopefully will it ever be.

In some cases, in-laws, or the parents of an ex-spouse, may become a problem for the custodial parent. If you find yourself in this situation, begin by bringing the matter to the attention of your ex-spouse, who may be willing to intervene on your behalf. Any direct approach to the grandparents may be unwelcome, so this is always your best option. If your ex-spouse refuses to cooperate or support you in this matter, limit your interaction with the grandparents as much as possible. While they have every right to see their grandchild, and this should not be restricted, you can and should limit your own time with them for your peace of mind.

A Multitude of Challenges

Every single parent with an ASD child will find challenges and obstacles. Some will require solutions unique to the individual family. Some issues that can arise are:

- Preventing elopement or escape when the parent is temporarily unavailable is a high priority
- Having safety measures in place within the household, especially if upper stories or decks are accessible to the child, will help prevent accidents
- Protecting younger children from an older ASD sibling is important, as the older sibling's curiosity might put the younger child at risk
- If you have a four-door car, be sure that the back doors cannot be opened while the car is moving
- Financially providing for a family may be difficult for the single parent, and careful budgeting is needed

Working and Caring for an ASD Child

Do you feel you are working full-time at everything? You are. There are never enough hours in the day to do it all. We hear and read that we can do it all if we are more organized, so we continually try to be all, do all, and accomplish all.

The reality is that no one person can do everything. A single parent has the jobs of parenting, career, and maintaining a home, and these are all full-time jobs! How can anyone do all of these things and still find time to sleep? The answer is simple: They can't, and you can't either.

Alert

Attempting to do everything alone is just setting yourself up for failure. Do not hesitate to ask friends and family for help. Consider hiring a local teenager to mow the lawn or help with chores to ease the burden. You need to protect your own health!

Priority One Is Your Child

Meeting the needs of a child with autism is going to take a lot of your time, so everything else will have to wait. You will be working in your everyday life to integrate sign language or speech therapy, sensory skills, behavioral management, and other things a child with autism has to learn. You may be using a special diet or doing therapy as well as coordinating with the different professionals your child sees regularly.

 Question

How do I make a schedule my child can interpret?
One easy way is to buy poster board and mount it on the wall. Take photos of activities, such as your child brushing her teeth or making her bed, and put those on the poster board in order. Your child can reference this to stay on top of things.

Make your life easier by setting up a realistic schedule. Plan times for baths, medications, stories, and all of the daily and weekly activities in which you and your child engage. If you have a specific time you do things, you will not feel the stress of trying to remember what needs to be done. It is hard to concentrate on reading your child a story if you are simultaneously trying to remember your other tasks. Putting up a poster board with drawings of the activities that you need to do with the corresponding times will help you stay on schedule and help your child know what to expect.

Priority Two Is Your Job

Your second priority has to be your job. You have responsibilities to your job and although it is very hard to combine work with the single parenting of a child with a disability, it can be done. The first thing you will want to do is find the most dependable day care possible. It may be a family member or friend—someone in whom you have the utmost confidence.

Talk to your employer about the fact that you have sole responsibility for your child, and that this could infringe on your work hours. Don't be overly dramatic or appear as though you are seeking sympathy. Be matter-of-fact and businesslike. Emphasize that there will be as little interference with your work as possible and give an honest estimate of what kind of time you think you may miss each month or week. Perhaps a job-sharing option is available or your employer will work with you to help solve the problem in some other way. This is especially true if you have been with the company for a while; but even a new boss may show some flexibility.

 Fact

Employers want people who are willing to work hard and deliver quality work. You may find your company is willing to make allowances for employees who have special needs. Split shifts, working from home, and flexible schedules are some of the options that may be available.

When you are at work, give your job everything you have. Although it is difficult when you are tired, worried, or stressed to put your personal life out of your mind, force yourself to do it, and perform your job to the best of your ability. If you excel as an employee, your employer will be more likely to work with you when things come up that force you to take time away from the office.

It is also a good idea to look into options such as different shifts, different locations, or alternative ways of earning an income. If you have a skill or trade where you could be successful at home, this would be a possibility worth investigating. Perhaps your existing employer would consider letting you telecommute either part or full-time. Keep in mind that once your child is in school, it will be much easier to work on a schedule that meets everyone's needs. No problem is permanent; some are just more persistent than others and require creative thinking.

Priority Three Is Your Home

You have to accept that there will be times when the house is messier than you would like. *House Beautiful* isn't coming over to photograph, so just relax. No parent has ever been graded on how immaculate a house is; so don't even try to compete on that level. It is so easy to be caught up in the trap that the house reflects how well you are doing as a mom or a dad, and it simply isn't true.

Tend to the issues that keep the family safe. A clean bathroom and kitchen are important, but if all the towels aren't folded and you need to fetch one from the laundry basket, life will go on. Organize your schedule so that you aren't overwhelmed with a huge mess at the end of the week. Doing a little each night is much easier than trying to do everything on a Saturday.

Some simple timesavers can make your life much easier. There are many resources available, such as magazine articles, books, and websites that have tips on how to save time in the house. Research different ideas and use the ones that work for you. As a start, try the following:

- **Lighten up the kitchen chores.** Use paper plates except on weekends.

- **Make mealtime preparation faster.** Buy single-serving, ready-to-serve grocery products for your child unless he or she has dietary restrictions.
- **Create less laundry from the kitchen.** Use a vinyl tablecloth, as it is easier to clean than a cloth one, and use paper towels instead of dishtowels.
- **Eliminate the missing sock mystery.** Pin socks together as soon as people take them off so sorting is a quicker job.
- **Prevent doing unexpected laundry late at night.** Have at least two weeks' worth of clean underwear, pants, and pajamas for your child.
- **If you have a cat, buy a covered litter box.** Children with an ASD are often intrigued with the cat box.
- **Invest in a new laundry basket.** Find one with three compartments to separate laundry during the week will prevent having to sort it all at laundry time.
- **Give yourself a night off once a week.** Visit the local fast-food restaurant. It may have a playground where your child can burn off some extra energy in a safe environment.
- **If a dog might become a part of the family, plan ahead.** If you don't have a fenced yard, consider who will walk the dog or who will watch your child when that chore is necessary.

 Essential

One great timesaver is paying your bills online. You can create automatic payments of many of your bills on your credit card and then just pay your credit card bill each month. Many banks also have online services with bill-paying features.

The Parent and Child Team

Enlist your child's help with household chores as soon as she is old enough. Teach her how to use a feather duster. The job won't be done perfectly, but she will thoroughly enjoy the process and it will save some work. Children love to help empty wastebaskets and children with autism are no exception. Teach your child how to make her bed and pick up her own toys.

Many little chores will help keep the house clean. It will allow you and your child to work on something together. It is also a good time for a child with autism to learn some basic life skills that she will use forever.

Finding Reliable Day Care

For the parent of a child with autism, day care can be the most difficult obstacle to overcome. There is no question that day care for a child with a disability is hard to find and parents are at an extreme disadvantage when they don't have a "normal" child. All too often, inquiries into a day care will be met with an answer of "I'm sorry, we are not equipped to handle the needs of a child with autism." It can be incredibly frustrating.

 Essential

Schedule an appointment with the Health and Human Services office in your area. You can do this on the computer or by telephone. They have many resources available that may be helpful to you in finding daycare for your child. You could also talk with them about obtaining respite care.

There are no easy answers. Sometimes a family member can help. Grandparents, aunts, uncles, cousins, siblings, or extended family members are your best option. Talk to members in your support group, call your doctor's office, talk to the special education department at a local school, and contact local religious centers. There are options, but they can be difficult to find. Be persistent.

Word-of-mouth continues to be the best recommendation, so don't hesitate to ask people you know and trust. When you do get a referral, visit the day care center several times, or meet with the person who will be caring for your child. If possible, arrive at the day care unannounced so you can see how things are run without an advance warning. Ask for references and contact them. Never place your child in an environment about which you feel uncomfortable.

Dating and Future Relationships

Many single parents, particularly single moms, are unsure how to approach dating, or even if they should date at all. They are concerned about how a potential serious relationship would affect their child with autism. They are equally concerned about how another adult, who is not the parent, will feel about a child with autism.

Dating?

Dating after you have been divorced or widowed can be difficult even for a person without children, but is a major challenge for the single parent of a child who is on the autism spectrum. The whole process of setting up a babysitter, getting ready for the date, and wondering what you will talk about is almost enough to make you cancel the whole thing. It seems easier to crawl back into a sweat suit and spend the evening with the kids. After all, isn't that what DVDs are for? Is it easier to stay at home and watch films with your kids instead of venturing out on a date? Yes, of course. Is it the best thing for you? Absolutely not!

Many single parents justify a life of solitude by saying that it is the right thing to do—that they shouldn't bring a stranger into the family if there's a possibility it won't be permanent, or that more time away from the child is a bad idea considering how many hours they already spend at work—the list of excuses goes on and on. It is usually a false front to cover what one woman honestly admitted: "Who would want me? A woman over thirty with a disabled child? What kind of catch am I?" Men feel the same way; it is not an emotion exclusive to women.

You Are Worth It

This is where you sit down in front of a mirror and say out loud one hundred times, or as many times as it takes, that you are an individual worth knowing and loving. Autism is part of your family's life, but autism does not define you. Your child is not autism, and you are not autism. Your child has an ASD but he is much, much more than that.

When you begin to see your own self worth, then someone else will be able to see it, too. Every person you meet has issues in her life. Your issue happens to be a child on the autism spectrum.

The Possibility of a Stepparent

When a relationship turns serious, marriage may very well become a possibility. For all practical purposes, whether a couple decides to live together or legally marry, the result is the same. A commitment will be made by two adults to bring their lives together, and this is going to involve any children in the relationship. It will be of special concern to the parent of a child with autism.

A new partner is also likely to have many concerns, especially if he has no experience with special needs children. He may worry that he will not know what to do or how to handle this child. He may be concerned about whether he can be an adequate parent to a child he is not entirely sure he understands.

When adults commit to a second marriage and there are children involved, it is wise to talk to a counselor. Many times issues lurking in the background can come to the surface in a discussion with an objective third party, and fears can be put to rest. You can get advice and discuss concerns that either of you may have. It is also a good idea to bring the stepparent-to-be to the child's primary care physician to talk about the child's current and future care.

 Fact

> Some statistics report a 50 percent failure rate in second marriages. To keep that statistic from including you, ask your future spouse to attend support-group meetings with you. Your new partner then can ask questions he may not feel comfortable asking you. This should decrease fears.

The biggest mistake people make is to visualize all the potential problems and situations that could ever possibly come up in an entire lifetime, and imagine them occurring all at once. Remember: One step at a time. You don't have to solve it all in one day. This is where a counselor or the child's physician can be helpful. Once worries are stated aloud, they can be seen in the proper perspective.

Concerns of Moms

It is very likely you are the custodial parent of your child with autism or perhaps you have joint custody with your ex-husband. Regardless, it is the nature of the mom to feel that as far as her children are concerned, "the buck stops here." The responsibility for these children is not something any parent, mom or dad, takes lightly, but to most mothers it is of critical importance.

If you have joint custody, you have advantage of the time your child is with his father. This will enable you to have a social life or even develop a new relationship without involving your child. If you have sole custody of your child, or if you are widowed, it is a bit more complicated, but you shouldn't deny yourself a social life if that is what you want. It is still best to hold off introducing your child to a man you are dating until the appropriate time, so you will need to enlist help from family and friends. Your support group may also be able to help; many set up rotating schedules for moms to care for one another's children to solve this very problem.

In many ways, a child with autism quickly sorts out the kind of men you will date. If she can't warm up to him, is this man someone you want to be part of your life? Some moms use their child's reaction as a litmus test; if a child rejects a potential partner, he could have some inherent flaw. Likewise, if a man can't warm up to your child with autism, then he is probably someone to think twice about, although some children will not accept any new man. Your child is a treasure and any man you develop a relationship with will be lucky to know her.

Concerns of Dads

One advantage men have is that the biological mother of the child with autism usually has custody. A single dad's schedule is typically more within his control than the schedule of a single mom.

Men who are single fathers of children with autism also have some definite disadvantages. Women might perceive them as "mom-shopping" to care for their children. A woman might also fear the responsibility for caring for someone else's special-needs child, or worry that a man with the emotional and financial responsibilities involved in raising a special-needs child will be unlikely to want to have more children. She will also worry about having to deal with the presence of an ex-wife, a woman she will have to interact with even after the child becomes an adult.

It sounds trite and clichéd, but it is true: Love can conquer many things. No one has perfect parenting skills. No one will always do the right thing with any child. We all make mistakes. The important thing is the love within a family, and that is something that can never be wrong if it is given unconditionally.

CHAPTER 9

ASD and the Effects on Siblings

Autism affects everyone in the family. Perhaps no one feels this effect more than the siblings of the ASD child. Parents of the child on the spectrum are often so wrapped up in the issues surrounding autism, and understandably so, that they overlook the ways autism is affecting their other children. It isn't bad parenting; it is human nature. Raising children is a balancing act for parents as they try to meet everyone's needs and provide a complete childhood for each of their children.

Older Siblings

When an older child or a teenager has a new sibling, it is always an adjustment. When autism is diagnosed a couple of years later, this adjustment will be even more challenging. A child who is ten years older than the new arrival will view the family dynamics differently from a younger child who may not get the same amount of attention as he had previously.

New Considerations

If there are a significant number of years separating the older sibling from the child with autism, the younger child with autism may not have as much impact on the daily life of the older child. This is especially true if the older child is in high school, for example, and nearly ready to move out of the house to live on her own or to go to college. The older child may not be much involved with the daily trials of living with a child with autism.

However, the older sibling may have some concerns that younger children wouldn't think of. The older child likely recognizes fairly quickly that autism is going to be around for the rest of her life, and she may already be concerned about her role in taking care of an autistic sibling in several years. This will impact not only her life but the life of her future spouse and any children they may have as well. Autism affects everyone in a family.

Slightly Older Siblings

When a child's sibling who is two to eight years younger is diagnosed with autism or another spectrum disorder, it can affect the sibling in several different ways. Children have their own personalities and how they react in a given situation will depend on their age and maturity. There is no universal way children handle issues in their lives, although there are some generalizations that can be made. Understanding the mechanisms behind observed behaviors can assist you in helping your other children. Typical reactions can include the following:

- A sibling acts as another parent.
- A sibling pulls away from the family.
- A sibling attempts to "make up" for autism by being a "model" child.
- A sibling establishes his own identity through flamboyant behavior.
- A sibling struggles with anxiety or depression.
- A sibling feels resentment toward the child with autism.

Although this list is by no means all-inclusive, most siblings of children with ASD will fall into one of these categories. Just when autism itself seems more than any person can emotionally handle, parents can be overwhelmed by the realization that their other children have developed problems because of their younger sibling. But it is, in reality, a simple process of identifying the issues and addressing them one by one; tackling the entire situation at once isn't going to work. Dealing with one issue, one crisis, one dilemma at a time will work with a little practice. And it's okay to make mistakes.

 Alert

Children accustomed to their sibling with autism not participating in games are thrilled when interaction and participation begins. They also can become jealous because of the attention focused on the child with autism. Don't forget to praise your other children for their skills and achievements.

The Parental Sibling

Children who begin to act as another parent have both positive and negative issues to deal with. The positive side is the child's acceptance and involvement in the family. As that child matures into an adult, he will have compassion for people with disabilities; it will not be something that is foreign to him as it is to so many people. The downside is that the parents might rely on such a child heavily, and it is possible for that child to take on so much responsibility that he becomes overwhelmed and loses himself in the process.

Parents need to be vigilant when an older child becomes parental. It isn't a behavior to be discouraged, as families should work together and look out for each other. But it is important not to let a child take on so much responsibility that he becomes overwhelmed and loses himself in the process. A child who observes his younger sibling about to poke a fork in an electrical outlet and stops him is a good thing. A child who feels responsible for everything the child with autism does, may carry a life-long burden that could take considerable counseling to resolve.

Younger Siblings

Younger children who have a slightly older sibling with autism have much the same issues, though magnified. There is, however, one advantage for the younger child who has a sibling with autism: She will not have had to adjust to her older sibling's disability—she has never known her brother to be anything other than who he is. However, even when the element of adjustment has been removed, other challenges remain.

A child with autism, because of the very nature of ASD, demands more time, patience, and tolerance than a child without the disorder would ever have. The major problem? A child without the disorder can "get lost." It is so easy to postpone the needs of a "normal" child because of the heavy demands of an ASD child.

 Fact

Negative attention is better than no attention—or so it may seem to a child. It is especially true for the sibling of a child with autism. If your other children begin having behavior problems, review how much individualized time they get from you. Negative behavior can be changed into a positive outcome.

Jealousy and Resentment

It is important that parents go the extra mile to avoid jealousy and resentment from the child who does not have autism. Jealousy is a problem that begins subtly, but when the children reach their teenage years, it becomes a serious problem. Resentment is the result of jealousy, and a resentful teenager is a problem waiting to happen. The teenage years are challenge enough without having undesirable behaviors surface as attempts to gain attention occur. You can watch for signs in your children indicating if jealousy and resentment are becoming an issue. A child may:

- Request that mom and dad attend school functions alone
- Feel concern or embarrassment about having her friends visit for sleepovers or other activities
- Become more in need of physical contact with one or both parents, wanting closeness such as cuddling
- Express jealousy overtly; the phrase: "But he gets to . . ." is a definite sign of jealousy
- Argue excessively about chores and responsibilities
- Show behavior that indicates an obsession with her health

Competitiveness

It is also important to watch for competitive behavior. Competitiveness may be the first sign of jealousy. A child who goes out of her way to show the parents accomplishments and skills may be feeling that the child with autism is getting a lot of positive feedback for reaching what is perceived to be very small goals. A child without autism does not understand that finally speaking one or two words is an enormous victory and will not understand why such a fuss isn't made over her normal or above normal accomplishments. It is important to take the time to praise all of your children for each milestone or goal they accomplish throughout their childhood.

Other behaviors will surface that are unique to each child, and the parents are the best gauges of those actions. A little common sense, a deep breath, and thinking the problem through will usually guide a parent into a proper course of action. Contrary to what children think, moms and dads usually love their children equally, and it is the job of the parents to display that through their behavior. If the child with autism is taking more and more time and attention, a parent may unintentionally leave the other children behind. Don't hesitate to check yourself to be sure you are conveying the correct message to your family, and remember that it is never too late to change.

Growing Up Too Fast

If there is a child with autism in the family and another baby comes along ten years later, there are some unique issues to be faced by the family. This age gap frequently occurs when parents have put off having a second child due to the pressures associated with raising a child with autism.

When a sibling is much younger than the child with autism, the younger child will never know of any adjustment that had to be made in the family. This is simply life, the way it has always been, and the way it will always be. The main risk to a significantly younger sibling of a disabled child occurs through the maturing years.

 Alert

Safety is an issue for parents with a newborn. If a child with autism is not totally self-involved, she will be very interested in the new baby. Her curiosity, which is unlikely to be tempered with caution, could inadvertently cause harm. Parents should take extra safety measures to avoid accidents.

It is very easy to inadvertently cause a child to "grow up" too quickly. Even though they are several years apart, the younger child starts watching out for the older because it is the natural thing to do. This burden of responsibility is too much for a child to bear, and may be sowing the seeds of resentment that will bloom fully later in life.

Most children realize as they approach their young adult years that the sibling with autism will forever be a part of their life. Realization strikes that someday caring for their sibling may be their responsibility. It isn't necessary to bring up this topic; it will arise on its own when the time is right. And it is very possible that a child with autism will eventually live in a supervised group home or even live independently.

When a child is much younger than his sibling with autism, it is less likely that the disability will interfere in the activities of childhood. The family will have adjusted and found their own routine that the younger child will fit into. It would be wise to find respite care so that the younger child will have time with parents alone. Involving extended family is an option that is not only helpful but also supportive. As the family pulls together, a family life is created that is secure and comfortable for all members.

The Isolated Sibling

Some children will fail to form an attachment to their sibling with autism and may attempt to put as much distance between themselves and their sibling and family as possible. This happens more commonly in children who are introverted. Often, the cause is quite simple: These children are tired of living with autism.

It is important that a child who withdraws from the family because of autism be allowed to flourish on her own. These children may be susceptible to depression, and if so a therapist might be needed to address the issues of this child. It is very important that the parents spend time just with that child to enjoy activities and projects that are unrelated to autism. Parents also need to be clear, verbally and through their actions, that they do not feel the sibling is responsible for her brother. The less the child with autism impacts his sibling, the better the chances for both children to evolve a healthy relationship over time.

 Essential

Support groups for parents of children with autism can provide information on locating a support group for siblings. Check with your local chapter of the Autism Society of America or other organizations that have support groups. Your child needs to realize she is not alone. The Internet can also be helpful.

It is common for parents of several children, when one or more has autism, to make provisions they might otherwise never have considered. For example, one mother said she would have never allowed a television in a child's bedroom until autism joined their family. However, the reality was that the sibling without autism could never watch his favorite programs without the child with ASD constantly changing the channel and throwing a tantrum when his own television shows were switched. Making that one adjustment increased the peace in the family. As this mother said, "Choose your battles. My other child deserved to watch his own shows and I just take a little extra time to monitor how much and what he is watching."

The Social Impact of Having an ASD Sibling

Children who have a sibling with ASD usually have mixed feelings about their brother or sister. At times, having a sibling with autism affects their social life, and at other times, it is totally irrelevant. Like any brother and sister combination, it can be a rocky road laced with arguments and love, all at the same time. The sibling of the child with autism will claim his sister as his worst enemy or best friend, depending on the day. One thing is certain: It is always an adventure!

Peers

Some of the biggest problems siblings of ASD children face are issues within their own peer group. Your child, having the experience of a sibling with a disability, has a different outlook on the world from that of many children. It is not unusual for children, particularly in the middle and elementary school years, to hear other children tease or outright ridicule their sibling with autism. Parents should address this immediately, as the problem will only escalate and eventually alienate a child from his own peer group.

If a child is being singled out because of his sibling, it is important for the parents to contact the school system. In this case, it isn't enough to tell your child to ignore the teasing, for two reasons; your child will generally defend his sibling with autism and be on the defensive whenever interacting with his peer group. Additionally, the children doing the teasing will continue to be intolerant of people who are different from them and the cycle will continue. Do not hesitate to schedule a conference with counselors, teachers, or other school staff to address and put an end to the problem.

Family Events

Of course, you don't always have to keep your children apart from each other. Your children may find if they include their friends in family activities, they will be more accepting of their special-needs sibling than expected, and they may have worried for no reason. In one instance, a child who has a brother with autism just a year younger than she is had recently taken some verbal harassment over her brother having autism. Although she wanted her brother to attend a concert with her, she was worried about what would happen. Her solution was to have him join her entire family in attending her school band concert, but she asked her father to sit with her brother right next to the exit just in case things got out of control. A hasty exit prevented anyone from knowing about the tantrum that occurred twenty minutes into the concert.

Don't hesitate to ask your child what he might suggest as a way to solve situations that could arise during a social occasion. The goal is to make the sibling who does not have autism feel comfortable without leaving out the child with autism. Sometimes it is not appropriate to bring a child with autism to certain events, just as it is not appropriate to bring any children to some events, and a babysitter is the best option. But other situations, with some family brainstorming, can usually be worked out.

When More than One Child has ASD

There is a 3 to 9 percent chance that in a family having one child with autism, a second child will have autism or be diagnosed with a disorder somewhere on the autism spectrum. In some families, one or two cousins, aunts, and uncles also have ASD. Two families in the United States each have six children all on the autism spectrum. Studying families like this should help geneticists find some answers

Considering Future Children

It is difficult, if not impossible, to advise a couple on whether or not they should consider having more children if they already have a child on the autism spectrum. So many factors are involved and it is a very personal decision. It is not a decision a couple can rush into or let others make for them.

Genetics or Unknown

If the ASD your child has is a proven genetic disorder, such as Rett Syndrome or Fragile X Syndrome, genetic testing is in order to determine the risk factors for a future pregnancy. If one child has been born with a genetic disorder, the odds are high another will be as well. In this case a genetic counselor and perhaps family counseling can help you reach a difficult decision.

The cause of other disorders within the autism spectrum is unknown. They could be caused by genetics, the result of unknown disease processes, or something in the environment—the bottom line is: no one knows. No matter what testing is done, there is no way to know if another child would develop autism.

There are many cases of families with a child with autism who have a child with another developmental disability. For example, ADD/ADHD is common in the siblings of a child on the autism spectrum.

Mental, Emotional, and Financial Impacts

Not only should a couple consider the mental and emotional impact of having a special-needs child, they should also consider the financial and long-term issues involved with raising children on the spectrum. It is rare for private insurance companies to cover any treatment that is needed for autism and related disorders, but this situation should improve under the new health insurance law.

 Fact

If your child has private insurance and sees his doctor for a condition unrelated to autism, be *certain* that the insurance forms do not indicate the diagnosis of autism. If a child is seen for an ear infection, it is not necessary to include the autism diagnosis, which may block benefits, but under the new law it should not.

There are government programs to help parents who meet certain guidelines. SSI, or Supplemental Security Income, is a program managed by the Social Security Administration. It was put in place to assist blind, aged, or disabled individuals who meet certain financial criteria. Benefits are paid directly to families to help with the expenses of daily living. Autism is an automatic allowance for benefits if your family meets certain qualifications such as income level and value of assets.

Be certain before you apply for SSI that you are able to thoroughly document the diagnosis of an autism spectrum disorder by physicians, a child psychologist, therapists, and even school personnel. Regardless of a child's age, the school system should help with early intervention. Even if your child is under school age, contact the school district to find out what programs and resources are available.

It is also important to remember that financial planning must be in place to protect and provide for any special-needs children if a parent dies. Life insurance, trust funds, and wills that provide for guardianship of a child are not luxuries. They are necessary and must be kept up-to-date at all times.

It's Your Decision

There are many well-meaning people, such as extended family, friends, and in-laws, who often feel it is their place to advise a couple on their family planning. Although it is difficult, you must stress, very kindly, that this is a personal decision and let the matter drop. If people persist in advising you against your wishes, be firm but polite in asserting your right to privacy.

If you decide not to have any more children, be at peace with that and do not allow others to make you feel guilty or inadequate. Many people feel it is their business to advise other people on childbearing and raising their children. It is no one's business but yours; just politely thank them for their interest and change the subject. If you decide you do want more children, again do not let others spoil your joy. These decisions are yours; you and your spouse will make the best decision for your family.

CHAPTER 10

ASD and the Extended Family

Autism and its related conditions are often misunderstood by the extended family. Some of your relatives may not even have heard of autism, or, if they have heard of it, they may have misconceptions about it. Family members have various responses as they attempt to advise the parents and educate themselves in the process. Regardless of whether or not the family relationships are close, remember that even a close family can be torn apart by ASD. Understanding common reactions and how to handle them can prevent misunderstandings that are harmful to family relationships from occurring.

Grandparents

Grandparents can be the easiest or the hardest family members to deal with when a child is diagnosed with autism. Most of the time they are a blessing, because they will assist and provide moral support through the early years of a child's life. Most grandparents have wisdom gained from years of experience that has taught them what is important.

Those Who Are Helpful
There are no official statistics on how grandparents respond to autism, but most parents say they lean heavily on their child's

grandparents for support and wouldn't know how to manage without them.

Often it is the grandparents that raise the first alert that something is wrong. A grandparent may question whether the child can hear properly. Grandparents generally love and care deeply for their grandchild, but they are not there day in and day out, so they often spot the lack of development more quickly than do the people in the household who see the child every day.

Your parents can often be your best advocate and stress reducers. Grandma may come through and shine when mom herself is falling apart over the diagnosis. Grandpa may do what dads do best—try to solve all the problems.

If your parents do not live nearby or you just don't relate well to them, perhaps you have developed closeness with your spouse's parents. Either way, the support from grandparents can help you in countless ways.

 Essential

Grandparents may never have heard of autism and will need to be educated about the various problems. Books can be overwhelming, so a good idea is to make a list of "frequently asked questions" along with answers to give them. This will help the grandparents understand what you are dealing with and save you from answering the same questions repeatedly.

Those Who Are Difficult

It is extremely hard on families when the grandparents of a disabled child create difficulties, so if problems exist it is wise to look for the cause. Generally, one of two issues are at the center.

The most common reason grandparents relate poorly, or not at all, to a grandchild who is disabled is simply that they are baffled. They just don't have the vaguest notion of how they should act, what they should do, if they should make allowances and, if so, what kind and how much. They want to interact with the child but don't know how to get from here to there. It appears as though they are ignoring their grandchild, but the reality is that they are at a loss, trying to handle a situation for which they are ill prepared.

If you have a parent who appears to be ignoring your child, try to determine if it is because they are unsure of what to do. If that appears to be the case, you can help them become involved with their grandchild by guiding the way. Give them a copy of this book and other books you have found helpful. Gather current magazine articles covering autism. Above all, show them how to act with your child; if they see that autism isn't the worst thing in the world, they will learn how to interact and become more confident in that relationship.

Less commonly, and much more difficult to handle, is the grandparent who chooses not to accept a child with a disability. In addition to this attitude being a loss for the child, it creates resentment from the child's parents and can be a volatile trigger for arguments and disharmony within the family. Other children, who are treated normally, receive a distorted message and sense the dissension in the family; they can become tense and insecure. After all, they may wonder, would they be rejected, too, if something happened to make them "less than perfect"?

Solutions for Difficult Situations

Suggesting the grandparents see a counselor will only make things worse; it's bad enough, in the grandparents' eyes, that the child isn't perfect, but to suggest they have a problem will only create anger and bitterness. Most parents who have struggled with this situation have said that only some distance makes things bearable. Distance can help everyone cope.

If putting some distance between you and the situation is not possible, limit contact as much as possible. Your other children can still see their grandparents, but explain to the children that the activity or location they are going to visit is not appropriate for your child with autism. Although it is tempting to argue the point with the grandparents, you are not going to reach a solution; it is less stressful, and, in the long run better for all parties concerned to avoid the situation.

 Essential

When grandparents don't try to understand autism, their attitude can be painful and upsetting. If you know you are never going to be able to change them, there is no need to make your other children feel uncomfortable or awkward. The children will usually sense there is a problem and withdraw from their grandparents.

The Unique In-Law Problem

In this case, a problem doesn't exist between the in-laws and the child with autism, but rather between the parents and the in-laws. There are no hard and fast rules on when this problem occurs, but there are some definite trends.

Mom and Her Mother-in-Law

When family relationships are strained, the most common problem is that between the mother of a child with autism and her husband's mother. Sometimes the relationship with a mother-in-law can be touchy even if there is not a disabled child. There also may be a special relationship, so much will depend upon the bond that existed prior to the diagnosis. If the relationship is strained to start out, and a grandchild is diagnosed with autism, a bad situation is exacerbated and the entire family can feel tremendous stress. Mom may find every decision or treatment being questioned by her mother-in-law. Raising a child with autism is challenging enough without having to defend every decision to your husband's mother.

If you have a problem with your mother-in-law, ask your husband to talk with her, or both of his parents together, to work toward a solution. If he won't, or it does no good, handle the situation with as much grace as possible and avoid as many interactions as possible. It is not good for you to feel stressed and resentful at every encounter with your mother-in-law. It is also not good for your children; if you are being questioned on decisions and choices you make for your family, it undermines your authority as a parent.

 Alert

> If either set of parents question your decisions about your children, assert your parental authority. When questions are asked, assume they are from concern, but if you feel you are being doubted, stand your ground. Don't allow anyone to cause you to doubt yourself.

Dad and His Mother-in-Law

The old jokes about in-laws have always centered on a man's mother-in-law, which is usually an unfair commentary on a woman's mother, but when it is a difficult relationship, the jokes ring all too true. This is only magnified when a child is disabled with a condition and the cause is unknown. Couple that with the lack of any definitive treatment and a tense situation can be the result. The mother may blame autism on genetics, even when there is no definitive cause established—and, of course, it will be the fault of the father of the child because of his bad genes. This is also sometimes used as a justification for saying, "I told you marrying him was a mistake."

When a dad has this problem, his wife needs to talk to her parents. A father of a child with autism has his own issues to deal with as he tries his best to juggle career, kids, and other activities. The last thing he needs to add to his plate is a challenging mother-in-law who questions his very existence in her daughter's life.

Other Family Members

Mothers-in-law are not the only family members that can make relationships uncomfortable. There are aunts, uncles, cousins, nieces, nephews, and even grandchildren involved in an extended family. And if a family is very large, there will be a great number of people related only by marriage who are involved as well. It can bring to mind the film, *The Good, the Bad and the Ugly*.

The Good

Fortunately, this is the most common situation for parents of children with autism and their extended family. Every family has its trials and tribulations, but when a family can work together for common goals, everyone benefits. If your extended family enjoys a good relationship, it will only help your child with social and interpersonal skills.

If your family is supportive and helpful, involve them in activities as much as you can. They can help with autism awareness functions you may be involved in. They are an extra set of eyes at a picnic to ensure your child's safety. Above all, they are a wonderful support system for the immediate family of a child with autism.

The Bad

Usually when a situation with extended family is not ideal, it is because of lack of involvement. This is a two-way street. Parents may decide not to participate in family events because they haven't figured out how to manage autism easily or because they feel unwelcome. Either way, the result is the same. The family that has a child with autism becomes isolated from the extended family.

If you consider your extended family ties to be less than ideal, try to figure out why. Is it a self-imposed exile, and is it possible that no one knows what to say or how to act with your child? A little education about autism can make the unknown less intimidating. Most people in a family want to get along and be together; they may need your help to achieve that with your child. Ignoring the issues won't change or make them go away, but addressing them directly can improve the situation.

The Ugly

Situations between family members can become very ugly when people in families have negative feelings toward one another and feel a need to express those feelings. This is especially true when autism is used as the vehicle. And it does happen.

If the relationships in your family are hostile or saturated with bad memories, you may not be able to work through the situation. Using autism as a pawn in interpersonal relationships is not good for you or your child and must not be allowed to happen. Your first priority is your own family and you have to do what is necessary to protect them.

Celebrating Family Holidays

Just about the time you have an established routine that works, a holiday comes along. Some are more disruptive than others, but all are something different from the normal day. Learning how to cope with various holidays can make them more fun for your family, and all you need to do is a little planning ahead. When you know a routine is going to go out the window, make a Plan B so you, at least, are prepared.

Spring and Summer Holidays

Several holidays during the warmer weather are usually enjoyed by families and should continue to be enjoyed even after autism is a part of your life. Having a child with autism should not change this. Planning and being aware of issues that may over stimulate your child can ward off many potential problems.

Mother's Day and Father's Day are two dates that parents can use to teach a child about giving to others. This is also an opportunity for a couple to demonstrate to the children their mutual respect and love. Dad giving Mom a Mother's Day gift—one that isn't a toaster or pancake griddle—teaches the children that Mom is a person, too. This is an important lesson for a child with autism to learn. As these children tend to "use" other people as tools, any opportunity to show that people are individuals to be respected and loved is an opportunity not to be missed.

Autumn Holidays

For most children, there is only one holiday in the fall that matters: Halloween. October 31st is a day to dress up and collect enough candy to give them tummy-aches until the next trick-or-treat date comes along. Remember, however, that some children do not like Halloween because the costumes and hordes of children scare them. For the parent of a child with autism, this holiday presents some extra challenges.

 Essential

Put reflective tape on your child's costume or clothing so you can spot her easily should she get away from you. Bright-colored costumes are helpful in finding your child in a group of costumed children; avoid the most popular costume of the year, as there will be many of those worn by children, and it can be confusing.

How does a parent explain to a child who is struggling with communication and conceptual skills not to take candy from a stranger, but then allow the child to march up to a strange doorway and ask for candy? If a child is on a special diet to treat autism, how do you explain to that child that all the other children get candy, but she doesn't? And how do you keep your own little goblin straight in a swarm of ghosts, bogeymen, and skeletons?

Unfortunately, there are no easy answers. Some parents only take their children trick-or-treating in a controlled environment, such as a shopping mall. Others go only to the homes of people they know.

Regardless of how you handle this holiday, be consistent year-to-year. Although it seems like a big gap between the dates, your child will hopefully learn that Halloween is a dress-up day, and a routine will be established. The Halloween costume may be worn for about a month, but for the fun it gives that is a small price to pay.

Winter Holidays

Although many holidays change our daily routines, there are none quite like those from Thanksgiving to New Year's. The activities that the holidays bring can turn a child's world topsy-turvy. Most children adapt well to this, as they are just as caught up in the excitement as the adults. But for a child with autism, the change in routine is not only unwanted, it is upsetting and can cause behavioral issues.

Some of the events that arise during the holiday season are predictable—so predictable that most parents don't even think of them as being upsetting. Some unusual events include:

- Parents may go to parties, meaning a babysitter will be needed.
- A visit to Santa for photographs each year is a common activity for many families.
- Friends and family may "pop in" for a visit unannounced.
- Carolers outside your front door are a total mystery to a child with autism.

- As families buy presents, the time spent in stores and shopping malls is greatly increased.
- Regularly watched television shows are often pre-empted for Christmas programs.
- Winter vacation may mean school is out of session for up to two weeks.
- There is a sudden influx of gifts, a decorated tree, and holiday baking.

All of these and many more holiday events individual to each family are enough to upset anyone's routine. But for the child with autism, they can cause total upheaval and overstimulation. Involve the child in decorating the tree; it may be the most unique and perhaps bizarre tree you will ever see, but it is a delightful and memorable way to celebrate.

 Fact

As the holidays get into full swing, remember that children with autism have their own special talents and abilities to contribute, and even though their creations may not be traditional in nature, they are things of beauty, things to be treasured, and remembered for a lifetime.

When over-stimulation becomes an issue, and it will if your family is more active during the holidays, the best advice a parent can follow is to "go with the flow." Use common sense—don't visit Santa during the busiest part of the weekend. Find a way to do your holiday shopping without having to take your child to the mall—buy most of your gifts online or order from catalogs.

Christmas is a holiday that all children figure out very quickly. As with Halloween, they will build a new routine, as they will understand that a Christmas tree means presents, and presents mean fun. Some adjustments will have to be made, but Christmas will be just as fun, or even more fun, than ever. Trust yourself and follow your instincts; if your child appears to be over-stimulated or agitated, slow things down.

Special Occasions

One challenge every family faces is the normal interaction and activities of social events and occasions. The following is not a complete list, of course, as every family is unique and has its own special activities. But many of these events are common to most families and can be problematic for a child with autism:

- Weddings
- Bridal showers
- Baby showers
- Graduation ceremonies
- Family picnics
- Family reunions
- Camping trips
- Birthday parties
- Anniversary parties

Participation in these events can be stressful for the entire family when a child with autism is having behavioral issues. And anticipation of these events can be equally stressful, making matters worse. Fun events become dreaded, and important gatherings are often missed.

If at all possible, continue attending family events. For both the immediate family and the farther-flung relatives, interacting with the child with autism at these events will help them feel involved and ultimately more comfortable with the situation.

 **Essential**

If a family member has passed away, particularly one who was close to your child, alert your child's teacher and therapists. Your child may exhibit behaviors that will surprise everyone if they are not aware of the situation. Children with autism may not directly express their grief, but it is present.

Funerals

A death in the family can present unique concerns. Because concepts are difficult to understand for people with autism, and death is a difficult concept for anyone to understand, your child with autism may be troubled by a funeral. Acting-out behaviors are common in these situations. Children with Asperger's or high-functioning autism may have a grasp of the situation, and in that case, parents should follow their instincts. Funerals are often disturbing even to children who do not have autism so leaving all the younger ones with a baby sitter may be the best idea.

Having autism in the family may change your interactions with your extended family, but if you plan ahead and prepare, those changes can be positive for everyone involved.

CHAPTER 11

Dealing with Society

P arents of a child with autism become very familiar with the behaviors of their child. Society, however, is still not accustomed to this disorder. The number of children affected with ASD is increasing, but many people have not interacted directly with a child who has autism. The majority of children appear to be perfectly fine, as their appearance is no different from that of any other child. When an apparently "normal" child begins to exhibit bizarre or out-of-control behaviors, challenges, which are victories waiting to happen, can't be far away.

Shopping

As mentioned earlier, one of the biggest challenges a family faces is the shopping trip. The weekly grocery shopping is necessary, but a trip to a shopping mall is often considered more trouble than it is worth. Variety stores are also an environment that can be difficult for not only the parents but for the child with autism as well.

The Grocery Store

It is always an adventure to go grocery shopping with children and this is especially true with a special-needs child. Although a Saturday morning cartoon advertising 800 varieties of breakfast cereals does not sway them, kids with ASD know what they like.

And what they like, they want. And when they want it, they want it now!

The easiest way to avoid the grocery store trauma and it is a trauma most of the time, is to avoid taking your child at all. How much easier it is for you to have your spouse watch him or get a babysitter during the time you need to shop! But there is a practical side to taking your child grocery shopping, even though it is harder for you. Shopping is a basic skill that needs to be learned. It often takes years for a child with autism to learn how to shop, and it is a skill that will help your child become more independent in his adult years.

 Alert

> If a child with autism wants something in a grocery store, he will simply put it in the shopping cart. He may not even know what it is, but the colors or shapes could attract him. Watch while your groceries are being checked out so that you don't accidentally buy unwanted merchandise.

Involving your child in shopping is one way to prevent battles over what goes into the grocery cart. For example, if you are going to buy a dozen apples, have your child select them and put them into a bag. As he is choosing the apples, guide him and show him that one has a bruise and isn't what you want, so he can learn. As he fills the cart, keep an eye on items such as bread that might get squashed, and help him arrange the cart. He may not seem to be taking it all in, but he is, and he will learn each time he visits the store with you.

One useful trick a parent can adopt to keep a shopping trip under control, particularly if it is a young child sitting in the cart's child seat, is to find a small, inexpensive toy for the child to play with while a parent shops. Handheld puzzles, travel toys, and action figures are good choices. Avoid noisy toys or those with many parts. And unless you want to be running all over the store, don't choose a ball. Children learn very quickly how to teach their parents to chase a ball.

The Variety Store

Shopping in variety stores—those huge one-stop shops—is a particular challenge for parents with children who have autism. When everything you could want is under one roof, it takes little time for a child to realize that the store contains many things *he* wants. Coupled with the sensory stimulation that a busy variety store supplies, it is a recipe for meltdowns and frazzled parents.

If you are taking your child with autism into this type of store, keep in mind that he may well experience sensory overload. The lights are fluorescent, and it is not unusual for people with ASD to see the blinking and flashing that most people cannot perceive. There are also many bright and colorful items within the store, and they will come rushing into your child's visual processing center all at once. If there is a great deal of noise from intercom systems, other children, and crowd chatter—these sounds will be painful for your child's ears. Don't be surprised if he covers his ears in such an environment. All of this sensory input can occur within seconds of entering the store, so before the shopping even begins, as a parent, you are already set up for a problem.

If you can avoid taking your child into this kind of store, it will be much easier. Once every few months is fine, but weekly shopping in a large variety store can be a very stressful experience. You are not depriving your child by leaving him at home, so you don't need to feel guilty for calling in a babysitter.

The Shopping Mall

Shopping malls are a mixture of good news and bad news. The good news is that there is enough to keep a child entertained, and the bad news is that, like other kinds of shopping, your child is likely to be overstimulated. Going from store to store to store is enough to confuse anyone; for a child with autism it can be far too much.

 Essential

If your child has a service dog, that dog is legally entitled to go anywhere. If you are denied access, speak with a manager. Be certain that the dog is trained well; he helps your child and you have become an ambassador for the benefits of a service animal.

School Functions

There are two types of school functions parents have to deal with when they have a child on the autism spectrum: those that involve the child and those that involve the child's siblings. Each offers opportunities for your child but can also create difficulties. Either can make you wonder who ever invented after school functions.

In the Spotlight

If your child is in special education, he may not be involved in many school functions such as concerts and plays. But if your child is in inclusive education, meaning he has classes with the rest of his classmates along with some special-ed classes for specific needs, there will be more occasions for after-school functions. Many children with autism have an aptitude for music and do well in a school band. If your child participates in band and is able to function as part of the greater whole, it will be tremendously rewarding for him, as well as for you. The steps of progress may be slower for the child with autism than for other children in the program, but the victory felt as progress is made is a feeling like no other.

In the Audience

Much more commonly, your child will attend his sibling's school functions with you. Concerts, plays, band recitals, and athletic events are only some of the events you will probably attend over the years. Sometimes your child with autism will enjoy them, and it will be a pleasurable experience for everyone. Other times, it will feel like *Nightmare on Elm Street*, and although it may still be worth it in the end, it can be very stressful at the time.

Following much of the previous advice will be helpful for school functions. There is a lot of noise whenever school-age children get together and your child is quite likely to suffer sensory overload. Centering your child's mind on his music and coloring, or on whatever he finds of interest, will provide a better experience for all concerned. If the activity is something that your child enjoys, you will find him watching with great interest, and so much the better. This may become an interest for him to pursue as well. "I would have never considered bowling for my son," a mother said. "It seemed boring for a boy with autism, but my daughter had an after-school bowling party, and we needed to go watch her team play. My son was intrigued! We tried it later in the week and he loved it!" Had they not attended the bowling party with their son, they may have never known of his interest.

 Essential

Consider bringing a babysitter to school functions to be in charge of handling any situations that arise with your child or if he needs to be quickly removed from the audience. This will allow you to continue watching your other children's performances.

If the situation is not a warm and fuzzy, positive experience, don't throw in the towel. Sit near the exit, and be prepared to make a quick dash in case the experience is less than interesting for your child. Never let your other children feel embarrassed by the actions of their sibling; it is hard enough to cope with school and childhood without having to explain a sibling's actions.

Restaurants

Eating out in restaurants can be a challenge for the parents of a child with autism. That doesn't mean you should never do it. The most important thing to remember is that your child has autism; she is not autism. You can still enjoy many of the activities you have enjoyed as a family, or dreamed of enjoying; you will have to make modifications, but you haven't lost everything you love to do. You can still eat out at restaurants—you just have to be prepared.

Eating-Out Behaviors

It is important to teach your children appropriate eating habits; they need to eat balanced meals. They should learn this at home; a restaurant is not the place to enforce rules about eating that are likely to be met with resistance. If a child with autism refuses to eat anything round—and this is a common obsession with autism—it is not a good time to try peas as a side dish. A child with an aversion to round things, when presented with meatballs, melon balls, and round slices of carrots is more likely than not to decide her dinner would make adequate apparel for his parents. And throwing a plate of food at a parent is a sure way to get a lot of the kind of attention you don't want.

 Alert

> It would be wise to choose a child friendly restaurant and to go early, not on a Saturday night. This way there should be less noise and you will get faster service. Talking about where you are going or showing your child pictures of a family eating in a restaurant could be helpful. Bring along a favorite toy and a book.

To avoid problems, just order what your child loves and what you know she will eat. Grilled cheese and fries are a sure hit with a child. Chocolate milk can also make many things better and is very useful for calming an unhappy child. Cheeseburgers are always a success, as is spaghetti or macaroni. Eat in ethnic restaurants as often as you like, but for your own sanity, be sure they have a basic children's menu. Sushi is not going to be on the list of favorites for your child, and experimenting with new food is best done at home.

Go Out for Dinner!

Keep in mind some basic strategies for dining out. Don't let autism keep you from the things and places you enjoy. You can easily adapt and have a great time with your family. You can increase everyone's enjoyment of the experience if you:

- Choose a booth whenever possible, and have your child take an inside seat to prevent her from bolting.
- Unless your child is a water drinker, request that no extra glasses of water be brought to the table to prevent spillage.
- Have plenty of napkins available in case something is spilled.
- Remove salt, pepper, and all other condiments from your child's reach.
- If your child is exceptionally hungry, his behavior may become irrational before the meal is served. Request a side dish of mashed potatoes and gravy, or some other favorite, to be served immediately to raise her blood sugar or give her a snack before you leave for the restaurant.
- Don't let dessert items be brought to the table until everyone, including your child, has finished his meal.
- Don't worry about food spilled on your child's clothes; in the scheme of things, it is a small thing.

Vacations

Most families take a vacation once every year or two. Many parents of children with autism think that autism precludes them from taking a week or two away from home, but that simply isn't true. Vacations may pose challenges, but these issues can be confronted and the problems solved. When planning your vacation, always remember that your goal is to protect your child, not become so panicked that no one can enjoy the vacation.

There are two things to remember as you plan your vacation. The first is that you want to maintain the routine of your child, and the second is that maintaining the routine is probably going to be difficult. That may sound like a contradiction, but it is important for parents to remember that they should plan for the best, but be prepared to handle anything unusual that arises.

The Importance of Routine

People with autism thrive on, and depend on, their routine. Schedules are seldom veered from, the order things are done is consistent, and the way the day unfolds is predictable. While some children adapt well to a disruption in their routine, other children will not adapt at all, and behavioral problems can be the result.

As you plan your vacation, consider your child's routine each day. If possible, keep as much of that routine the same as you can. Getting up and having breakfast at normal times will start the day off on a better foot when the family is away from home. If your child is used to watching television in the morning, and you are in a motel or hotel with a TV, turn it on and find his favorite programs. If you are camping, find an activity that will distract your child from dwelling on his routine. Some families always go to the same child-friendly vacation spot, so their child with autism will be comfortable in the surroundings and look forward to the trip.

Airplane Travel

A trip by airplane may not be the best choice for a child who is prone to temper tantrums or meltdowns. However, if it is a necessity because of a move, a death in the family, or an important celebration, some suggestions could help.

First, check with the airlines to see if you can be permitted to board ahead of the other passengers. Some role-playing ahead of time or even a visit to an airport might also be a good idea. Reading a book about a child's airplane trip so your child can visualize the airport and airplane is another way to help prevent problems.

Be sure to take along some favorite small toys, a favorite pillow or blanket and a small DVD player with some cartoons or a movie. These could save the day. Some favorite snacks are also important.

 Question

How can I keep some semblance of a normal routine on vacation?
It is important to provide favorite meals. Eating is a big sensory experience and meals are pivotal parts of the day. If your child is used to having a grilled cheese sandwich or hamburger and fries at lunch, don't offer fish and chips instead.

Remember that no liquids can be taken through security and that medications must be in a small zip-top bag and should all be labeled. No knives, play guns, or sharp instruments are allowed through security.

Another wise idea would be to check with your child's pediatrician or child neurologist to see if some sedation should be prescribed in case your child gets out of control. Be sure that it is a medication you have used before since kids often react in bad ways to new medicines.

Using a Vacation as Sensory Therapy

Although a vacation is a time to "get away from it all," your child will still have autism. Incorporating different activities can provide sensory therapy for your child that he might not have otherwise experienced. Don't burden yourself with the idea of therapy; consider it part of the fun that you will have with your child.

Textures, sounds, sights, colors, and music are just some of the examples. Going to the beach and playing with sand is sensory therapy and so is walking through a forest and feeling the different varieties of leaves. Museums provide opportunities to identify colors and shapes. Your entire vacation is one big sensory supply package that can be used to provide therapeutic experiences and a lot of fun.

Another tip that all parents who have been on this road will endorse is to try and keep your child's sleep schedule the same. Most people tend to burn the candle at both ends on vacation, packing as much fun and activity as possible into their time. Children who do not have autism can handle this temporary adjustment in their schedule, but autism does not lend itself well to this change. If your child is exhausted, difficult behaviors will be hard to control, and the entire family will feel the stress of the ordeal. If you are able to stick to the daily routine your child has come to expect, your vacation will be fun and restful, not only for your child but for the entire family as well.

A Special Memory Scrapbook

One idea that will keep a child occupied and busy, as well as create a special memory, is to make a vacation scrapbook. Purchase a scrapbook with heavy pages, and nontoxic glue. It is also helpful to have clear, double-sided tape, glitter, stickers, and colorful markers. On the cover put your child's name and a photograph of the vacation spot you are going to visit.

During your vacation, help your child collect leaves, flowers, brochures, wrappers, photos, and other items of interest. Pasting or taping them into the scrapbook is a tactile experience and will journal the vacation. If your child is nonverbal, he can point to the mementos to let you know what he is thinking about, and this can also add to the use of sign language. Starting the scrapbook before you leave is helpful for communication; having photographs of things a child might need to ask for can prevent frustration for everyone. If your child can point to a picture of a bathroom, an accident can be avoided, and he will have learned another way to control his environment.

 Essential

A good idea is to take photographs of the family during the vacation and then put them into the book with everyone's names written next to the pictures. A child with autism is usually very self-involved and photographs that show him interacting with others will be helpful.

Bringing the Vacation Home

It is also fun on an outdoor vacation to bring along an empty coffee can to collect pebbles and rocks. Rocks have different colors and textures. Collecting them can provide a sensory exercise. It is also fun. At the ocean, your child can gather a variety of shells. No matter where you go, it is likely that something can be collected and used for a sensory exercise that also brings your child a lot of pleasure.

Collecting postcards is another way to integrate therapy into your child's life. The visual element will help him to remember the places the family visited on vacation. Punching a hole in the upper corner of each card and attaching them together with a ring or key chain makes these cards easy to view and talk about. This will allow you and your child to look at the cards and remember your vacation together.

CHAPTER 12

Starting School

The he first day of school is always exciting for both parents and children. For the parent of a child with autism, daily trips to school have probably been occurring for quite some time; they don't begin at kindergarten. In the United States, all fifty states are mandated to have early intervention programs and special education available to children. For children with autism, early intervention will most likely begin around the child's second birthday. Special education starts for children at the age of three.

What You Need to Know about the Law

The special education maze is complicated at times, and you may find yourself feeling like you're in an adversarial relationship with the school system. But never forget that you are your child's best advocate. Staying informed about political and legal issues that affect children with autism is critical to your child's successful school career. If you find it hard to speak up when you meet with school personnel, it is wise to take an advocate or even a special education attorney with you. Some agencies have these specialists available. If not, a more experienced parent of a child with autism might be willing to come along as your advocate.

IDEA

In the mid-1970s, a new law was enacted called the Education for All Handicapped Children Act of 1975. The federal government had finally recognized that inadequate education for children with disabilities was very costly for American society. In 1997, the law was given a major facelift and was renamed the Individuals with Disabilities Education Act (IDEA).

Title I is a federal funding program for public schools above a specific student population count. IDEA requires public schools receiving Title I funding to follow two standards: All students must have available to them a free appropriate public education (FAPE), and that education must be within the least restrictive environment (LRE). This education is to be provided from ages three to twenty-two, but may have variances based on individual state laws.

The Legalese of Special Education

Although it may feel as though you need to be an attorney or political science expert at times to understand the technicalities of the government's involvement with special education, it isn't all that difficult. Laws will come and go, change and modify, and evolve to better (it's hoped) serve our children. What is important is that you understand the basic principles of special education laws so that when changes do occur, as a parent you can interpret the effect they may have on your child. There are some changes under the new education laws passed by the present administration, but it may take a while for all of them to be implemented.

There are many newsletters and websites that provide current and up-to-date information on issues in the government that can affect special education. It isn't so important that you understand and are aware of every little detail but that you know how to handle the laws should you have problems with your child's education. No one can be an expert on everything, but anyone can be an expert on finding information they may need. Avail yourself of all of the experts to stay current on congressional issues that affect the rights of students with disabilities.

Integration and Special Education

When a student is disabled, education includes much more than the three R's. Beyond academic learning, students in special education programs also learn about managing the needs of their daily life. Activities of daily living (ADL) such as dressing, toileting, self-feeding, and other hygiene needs are also taught. The needs of a student in special education are similar in some ways to those of nondisabled students, but can also be very different. Thus a multifaceted program, coordinated by teachers, administrators, therapists, and parents, is planned annually. This plan is known as the Individual Education Program (IEP), which is discussed in more detail in the next section.

Least Restrictive Environments, Mainstreaming, and Inclusion

IDEA establishes that students must have access to an education in the Least Restrictive Environment (LRE). In practice, this means that a student must be placed in the same classroom she would attend if she were not disabled. Supplementary services, such as aides, support systems, and communication equipment, should be used to achieve this goal. If a student's IEP clearly shows that the regular classroom is not suitable, after thoroughly researching the use of various supports, aids, and paraprofessionals, other arrangements can be made. Inclusion, mainstreaming, and LRE all refer to the same thing.

However, IDEA has recognized that the regular classroom is not suitable for all students. It calls for a "continuum of alternative placement" to answer the needs of each child. This includes special education classrooms, special schools, or instruction in the home environment. In some instances a personal aide may also be necessary and would be required by law.

Achieving Free Appropriate Public Education (FAPE)

FAPE is something to which every child in the United States is entitled, even if it is a phrase very few parents know. Every child is entitled to have the best education possible, it must be easily accessible, and can have no attached fees. This includes services such as special education and "related services" necessary to fulfill the IEP goals. This mandate applies to all Title I schools and encompasses academics, physical education, speech therapy when needed, and occupational and physical therapy if these have educational benefits.

 Fact

The law says that no child shall be denied needed services because of lack of personnel. If the school does not have the necessary professionals, they are required by law to pay for outside services. You may need to be quite aggressive to have the school district pay for any outside services and might need an advocate to help you.

Related services relevant to FAPE include hearing evaluations, speech therapy, psychological counseling, physical and occupational therapy, recreational therapy, and vocational counseling. This is not an all-inclusive list, as any service necessary for a child's success is included in this category. These are not luxuries; they are essential to acquiring the free and appropriate public education that every child is entitled to, by law, in the United States. However, when there are budget problems, you may find that you will have to push hard to get some needed services and then will have to constantly check to be sure your child is receiving them. "The squeaky wheel does get the grease."

A free and appropriate public education means that every child with a disability is in essentially the same environment as he would be were he not disabled. Least restrictive environments are part of this education and related services are as well. FAPE and LRE or inclusion, as it is commonly known, are the tangible manifestations of IDEA.

Individual Educational Program

Individual Educational Program (IEP) is a term that you will need to know. Think of it as the road map that runs from early intervention through graduation. This plan describes in detail all special education services that will be called upon to meet the needs of your child with autism. Each IEP is different, because each student is different. It outlines goals and expectations for your child and gives you an idea of what to expect for the school year.

 **Question**

Can a parent ask for a new IEP at any time?
Yes. A parent has the right to call for an IEP meeting anytime she feels there are needs to be addressed or revisions that should be made. Children change over a twelve-month period and the IEP may need to change as well.

The IEP is a fluid plan, meaning it changes from year to year and sometimes even within the same year as different milestones are reached or as problems occur. It can also be thought of as a contract, as it commits the school to using resources to achieve the goals the team sets. A well-done IEP also serves to eliminate misunderstandings by all of the members of the educational team.

Without an IEP, there is no special education; therefore, think of this document as the single most important part of your child's education.

Traditionally short-term goals are part of every IEP. Long-term or annual goals in the IEP—the heart of the document—will be the baseline on which a child's education is planned. The goals that are to unfold over a twelve-month period must be reasonable, practical, and designed to strengthen a weak area that is of educational concern. It is important that these goals match the student's current level of performance; they should not reach too high or too low. Parents and teachers need to consider a child's abilities and how they can best enhance those for progress and maturity.

The IEP Team

The IEP team is made up of a group of people who work with you and your child to create the best education plan possible. Certain people are required to be involved. Other experts may be involved as well. The team includes:

- **The student**—In reality, it is unlikely that your child will be included in an IEP meeting, so it is your job as the child's parent to address his desires and concerns if he has expressed them.
- **The special education teacher**—This individual will be the one to oversee the plan that is established in the meeting.
- **A school administrator**—This will be either a principal or special education director.
- **An adult-service-agency representative**—This is only required if transition services are being planned that would involve an outside agency. If it is physically impossible for someone to attend, a phone conference will suffice.
- **An interpreter**—This is a requirement if the parents are deaf or do not speak English.

Other teachers and therapists may be asked to join the meeting if appropriate. Parents may also request an advocate of their choosing if they wish. It is very helpful to have an advocate, particularly if you are new to the IEP process. Parents must be notified of an IEP meeting reasonably ahead of time and if the date cannot be arranged with their schedules, the IEP must be rescheduled. If a parent is unable to attend—for instance, because she is serving in the military—the school is to make alternative arrangements through phone conference or another satisfactory method that will include the parent. An IEP meeting can also be taped if you give the school personnel adequate (at least twenty-four hours) notice that you intend to do this.

 Essential

The IEP meeting cannot take place without a parent present. Parents need to be involved and the school district must go out of its way to include them. It is now possible to have an IEP using video conferencing but it much more effective to have a meeting where all the involved professionals can be present.

The IEP Process

Your first IEP meeting may be intimidating. You will want to dress in a way that you will be taken seriously. You can bring a friend or advocate with you if you are feeling anxious about the meeting. A conference is usually called by the school, but can be called by anyone who feels a meeting is necessary. If a parent requests the IEP, IDEA states that it must be conducted within thirty days from the date the request was filed with the special education department.

IEP meetings take place at the school or a school district office and will include the entire IEP team. This includes parents, teachers, administrators, and anyone involved (even a member of the lunch-room staff isn't out of the question if a child has dietary issues). The entire process can be unsettling to parents, as this large and structured meeting can emphasize the severity of their child's disorder. But remember that this team has been created to help your child acquire the best education possible, and you are a team member—with equal ranking and qualification.

As a permanent record, all parties will sign paperwork acknowledging the meeting date and time and you will sign a form that acknowledges you have a copy of the special education laws and that you know the rights of you and your child.

The meeting itself will cover all of the team's goals and expectations for your child. You and the team will go through various categories of his education, such as communication skills, and rate his current levels of performance. Goals will then be established to work on for the next twelve months. This process will continue for each service your child needs.

 Alert

Schools may have their school psychologist do any necessary testing. However, school psychologists may have time and experience limitations. It could be important to have an outside child psychologist do testing to decide what services your child needs and the best way he can learn. If you do not have an official diagnosis and intervention at school is being delayed, consult with a child psychologist, a pediatrician with a special interest in autism, or a developmental pediatrician.

It is helpful for parents to bring a list of questions and goals to the IEP meeting. If you feel that the school should provide particular services, this is the place to discuss it. Even if the school personnel do not agree with your requests, they must address them. For example, a school that will not provide sign language instruction at the parent's request needs to have a very good reason for denying it. A speech therapist should be present to talk about the reasons for and against. Lack of personnel or schedule concerns are not good enough excuses. If you do not agree with the findings decided on at the IEP, it is not necessary for you to sign the document; or you can sign it but write your objections next to the items with which you disagree.

The IEP meeting should be held every twelve months. As it comes time to plan the next year's IEP, parents should think about the progress their child has made over the past twelve months. Step back and observe your child's behavior, speech, and social skills. Be as objective as possible. If you feel he is progressing at the rate expected, you know the IEP is working. If he isn't progressing, the IEP needs to be revisited with changes made to help your child. If parents move to another school district the previous IEP should stay in place until a new IEP or testing have taken place.

 Alert

Reports from professionals in private practice, who have examined your child, must be read and discussed at the IEP meeting. You may have to be quite assertive to make this happen. The school authorities may be particularly uncomfortable about including the report of a private child psychologist who has tested your child, but they must do so.

Further Education

When your child reaches the age of fourteen, under the IDEIA law, a school must begin to make a transition plan for your child. This is called an Individual Transition Plan. The first half of a transition plan is to determine your teen's goals. If your child is able to communicate his hopes for his future, these should be part of the transition plan. The second half addresses how the school will provide an education that will assist your child in meeting those goals. Any needed transition services must be written into the IEP including a plan about how the goals will be met. You can invite individuals from outside agencies or community organizations to the meeting. In your teen's senior year, a counselor from the Department of Vocational Rehabilitation can be invited to assist in planning for job training or any special college programs. Transportation needs should also be addressed.

Identifying Your Child's Interests

As children reach their teenage years, most start expanding their horizons to include special interests. This can also be true for teens with autism, if they have direction and supervision to help them explore the possibilities. It's important that parents help develop interests and talents in their teen. Settling for a future with little opportunity for fulfillment is not a desirable option.

How do you determine the interests and talents that may be hidden in your child? If you don't have a computer at home, get one and load it with drawing, reading, and math software as well as other software of interest to young people her age. Avoid the video game model involving repetitive activity that puts a child into a trance-like state; autism has enough of that without adding more. The games and activities that will stretch your child's mind are valuable.

You may discover that your child has a talent in graphic arts, or that math is second nature to her. You may find she knows more about computers than you do! Many people with autism are finding their way into technology fields because of the home computer. This is an especially strong field for people with Asperger's Syndrome.

Another option for you to find your child's abilities is the time-honored tradition of "bringing your child to work" day. It doesn't have to be your place of employment; any activities you are involved in may be of interest to your child. She can garden with you, file movies and books, help you paint a wall, or wash the car.

Anything you do is something your child might be interested in, and it will give her a bigger window to see the world. It could also provide your child with a doorway to walk into the world.

The Traditional Educational Path

Some children with autism continue with traditional education throughout their school career. They may go on to college and become very successful in a chosen field. Having autism does not preclude a college education and a career. Some people with autism have earned their doctorate degrees and become leaders in their field.

The two primary methods used to instruct children with autism are applied behavioral analysis (ABA), and Treatment and Education of Autistic and Related Communication-Handicapped Children (TEACCH). There are supporters and detractors of each method; neither method is right or wrong, as what will work for one child may not be suitable for another child. Parents need to understand both methods and decide which is best for their child.

The TEACCH Method

TEACCH is the most commonly used method for the instruction of students with autism. Your school system may not use the term TEACCH for the structure they have in the classroom, but it is easily identified. It can be less intensive and therefore less stressful, especially for younger children.

 Essential

Some critics of the TEACCH method feel that it does not emphasize socialization and verbalization skills enough. Additionally, no long-term studies have been done to determine the program's value. So as a parent you need to get a great deal of information before involving your child in the program.

The basis of TEACCH is visual learning and structure. The traits of autism are thus used to the instructor's advantage as well as to the student's benefit. Visualization is a powerful tool for people with autism and can be used in a child's learning. TEACCH uses schedules that are posted in various locations to help a child associate a picture with an activity; this helps with learning the usefulness of words as well as in creating a reliable routine. You can learn more about the TEACCH program on their official website: *www.teacch.com.*

The ABA Method

ABA was developed using the principle of positive reinforcement. Skills are taught to a child and when the skill is performed correctly, the child is rewarded, reinforcing the desired behavior, skill, or activity. Chapter 17 covers ABA therapy in more detail. Behaviors that are desirable for a child with autism to learn, such as eye contact, imitative behavior, and language, are taught at first. When the child has mastered these skills and can use them as a foundation, instructors then teach skills that are more complex.

Bullying

When a child seems different or is not able to defend himself, bullying by other kids is always a worry. If your child comes home with bruises or seems unusually upset, bullying could be the problem. The first step would be to talk to your child's siblings and any of your child's friends. Then if you cannot get answers, talk with the teacher or classroom aide. If that is not satisfactory, you might volunteer for a few times on the playground so that you can observe firsthand what might be going on. If you still don't have definite proof of bullying, speak with the school principal. If the bullying continues, you may need to request an IEP with an advocate or even a special education attorney present.

Bullying can be extremely dangerous and can occur both in and out of school. Your instincts as a parent should let you know if bullying is occurring so don't be afraid to be aggressive in finding out what is going on. Sometimes too, a teacher or an aide can bully a child. This can be a delicate situation. If you hear reports that this is happening, you may have to choose a different school or a different class for your child.

Parents' Expectations

If you can get through your child's time at school without at least one major battle each year, you will have the respect and envy of every parent of a child with autism. Keeping your goals and expectations positive and realistic can minimize the battles.

There is a new PTA for you to join. Not the one at your child's school but the one that stands for:

Parent Teacher Advocate

You have by now earned the right to use all three titles. You know you are a parent, and you may have figured out that you are your child's first and best teacher as well. You are also your child's best, and sometimes only, advocate. Running interference is just part of being a parent and it may be the first line appearing in the job description as a parent of a child with autism.

CHAPTER 13

Child to Teenager

Puberty, teenagers, adolescence. These are all words many parents dread, and it is no different for the parent of a child with autism. Many of the issues that arise during the teen years bring up questions and concerns that may be difficult to solve. However, because many kids diagnosed with autism are now in their teens, more information is available to make this time in a family's life easier. Teenage years can be fun for teens with autism as well.

Physical Changes of Puberty

Puberty! That word can put chills up and down the backs of even experienced parents of kids not on the autism spectrum. It is a time of changes, of testing the boundaries; a time of becoming mature, but acting immature; and a time of experiencing the world. For a teen with autism it is all those things and more. Many changes happen to a teen with autism when puberty arrives. Some are physical and others are emotional and mental.

Autism-Related Changes

If a teen is prone to seizures, this time in his life will likely indicate the role seizures will play in his future. If he has not had seizures previously, he may begin to have them at puberty. If he already has them, they may increase or could cease. If the frequency of your teen's seizures changes, consult with your pediatric neurologist. She may wish to make medication changes.

Bowel function can also change at this time. A child who has had encopresis may suddenly be "cured." Bowel habits may become more regular and comfortable. Be sure to discuss any concerns with your teen's physician. If your teen continues to have problems with bowel function, stool softeners and an increase in water and foods containing fiber can be helpful.

Dealing with Other Changes

Most new issues you will face when your teen reaches puberty are the same ones that any parent of a teen faces, but they can be harder to deal with if your child has autism. Acne is often an indicator of the hormonal changes in puberty, and it is difficult to get children to care for their skin. It is important, however, that this be done, as a child with severe skin eruptions is even more isolated from his peers. Establish a routine that keeps your teen's skin clean and free of oil and bacteria; cleansing pads are good for this purpose. An appointment with a dermatologist may also be helpful.

If you haven't seen the reality of "growing pains," you may become aware of them now.

If your child seems irritable or tends to absently rub his arms and legs, be suspicious that "growing pains" may be the problem. Try to relieve the discomfort with some medicine your doctor recommends. Plenty of calcium is important at this stage in a teen's life, so if your child does not drink milk, consider a calcium supplement if suggested by your teen's physician.

Other physical changes are normal and natural but may confuse your teenager. Body hair begins to appear, boys' voices crack, girls develop breasts—your teen wakes up in a new and unfamiliar body. If you find your teenager analyzing his or her body, ignore it. The novelty will go away and if you draw attention to it, you will inadvertently reinforce the behavior.

Emotional Changes of Puberty

Even more dramatic than the physical changes are the emotional and mental changes that a teenager experiences as she abandons childhood for adolescence. Autism is isolating and puberty can complicate the situation.

It is the parent's job to make certain that their teenagers continue to do the things they are capable of doing for themselves. It is true that a teenager with autism may not be interested in the latest fashions the kids are wearing at her school, but mom and dad need to be sure their teen chooses appropriate clothing. Your teenager may not care about the latest haircut or even whether she has taken a shower, but you need to emphasize the importance of cleanliness and good grooming. A teenager's world turns on social acceptance, and since kids with autism struggle with social interaction, they will need all of the help they can get at this age.

Other emotional changes can include fragile feelings, willfulness, belligerence—your teenager may experience the complete range of emotions any adolescent has on entering puberty. If your teen is inclined toward aggression or anger outbursts, do not be surprised if the nature of those outbursts changes. Some teens have fewer outbursts while others have more than they did before puberty. It is common for a teenager to have fewer but more intense outbursts.

Sexuality

It is difficult for parents when any child grows from the relative innocence of childhood to adulthood; sexuality is a topic that requires education, explanation, and understanding. It can be bewildering and even frightening for a child. But when the child has autism, the problem is magnified. How does a person with autism express her sexuality when her social skills are challenged?

Mom and Dad, You Need to Talk

This is the most important thing you can do for your child. Both of you need to sit down together and talk about how you feel about puberty, adolescence, sexuality, and the role of sexuality for your children. It is important that you agree on issues of such importance. Individuals with autism will have unique as well as diverse problems with sexuality. The only common thread all those on the autism spectrum have is that their problems with socialization affect their behavior. How those behaviors are expressed is like a snowflake; you will never see two that are alike.

 Essential

Many adults are uncomfortable about dealing with the sexuality of their children. Parents need to put those feelings aside so that they can have a dialogue about this subject. If the conversation is delayed, you may find yourself facing an even more uncomfortable conversation after a bad situation arises.

What if your child with autism is unable to experience sexuality? Coming to terms with the fact that marriage or children might not be possible is another loss for a parent struggling with the diagnosis of autism. When parents realize this part of their child's life may be diminished or nonexistent, it becomes another loss—another item on the list of things their child will not experience. Openly discussing your concerns about these issues will help both of you prepare for what is to come.

Some people with autism do not have a sexual drive and if that is the case, there is no reason to try to change this. Some medications can cause a loss of libido; other times the cause is unknown. Given the problems a person with autism might encounter with sexuality, a lack of sexual drive could be a blessing in disguise.

Understanding Sexuality

A person with autism who has a functioning libido will have difficulties expressing his sexuality in an appropriate manner. Matters of disease prevention, sexual abuse, birth control, and behavior management are difficult to explain to a young person, or an adult, who struggles with understanding concepts. As with the other things in your child's life that you have had to control, if the autism is severe enough to limit judgment, you need to take control of the sexuality as well. If it is any consolation, it will be harder on you as a parent than it will be on your child. No one wants to deny their child a life full of love and experiences, but sometimes it is the only choice available.

"Informed consent" between two adults is the generally accepted measure of whether a sexual activity is appropriate. Understanding what informed consent is will help you as a parent to assist your child as he grows up. There can be no informed consent unless each individual can:

- Understand and communicate to another person the word or the meaning of the word "no."
- If given different choices, demonstrate the ability to make a choice based on available information.
- Understand that there are appropriate places and times for sexual behavior.
- Understand and detect danger and threats in order to react properly.
- Understand the word "no" and be able to cease an activity if told to do so.

There are many more factors involved in determining a person's ability to make an informed choice, but if a teenager lacks these skills, he is not capable of making sexual decisions for himself. And even if a teen communicates well and clearly, social interactions may still be beyond his grasp. Saying "no" does a person little good if they don't know when to say it.

Fact

It is wise when working on an IEP with school personnel to include these issues. It is important that they know you are aware of potential problems with your teen's sexuality. It is also helpful for the teachers and aides to work on helping your child to understand when saying "no" is appropriate.

Unwanted Sexual Advances

Parents need to consider the risk factors as they make decisions regarding their child's sexuality. HIV/AIDS is a risk for any kind of unprotected sexual contact involving body fluids. Children with autism are also easy targets for sexual abuse, as they do not always understand dangerous, threatening, or inappropriate situations. Parents should not let themselves be ruled by fear, but they need to become proactive in the protection of their children.

Children and adults with autism have every right to friendships and relationships. If parents are in charge of their child's sexuality, their goal should be to help the child understand sexuality as much as possible to prevent the child from becoming a victim of unwanted sexual activity. When a child has a sexual experience against her will, or without her understanding, it is very hard on the entire family.

Menstruation

Considering what a frightening thing the onset of menstruation can be for a girl, it can be much more so if there are communication deficits. It may be natural, but it is still blood, and it can be alarming. The transition for girls with autism can be difficult, but it can be done. All that's required is sensitivity and some education.

Indications of Menarche

The best way to help a girl beginning her menstrual cycle is to be prepared ahead of time. Watching for the signs that show your daughter is entering into menarche will allow you to teach her as much as possible about what is happening to her body and prepare her for what is to come.

When girls enter puberty, one of the first indications may be their behavior. Parents will notice irritability, which will be difficult to distinguish from the irritability or angry outbursts associated with autism. It takes little to provoke a bad mood in a prepubescent girl, and outbursts of anger are common as well. Things that were once loved are now a source of embarrassment. But how do you recognize the arrival of puberty in a child when irritability and outbursts have always been part of the daily routine?

 Essential

One helpful aspect of the menstrual cycle is that it can often be charted, although beginning menstrual periods may be quite irregular. People with autism often like to use a calendar, loving the structure of the routine, and if a girl's cycle is regular this can help parents plan for any problems.

It is important for parents of girls with autism to be attuned to their daughter's behavior. Routines can now be your best friend—even though you may have felt a slave to them in the past, they can help you be aware of what is going on with your daughter. If you notice that things are upsetting her that didn't six or twelve months ago, and you see a hair-trigger temper, that is a warning sign.

Breast development is usually the first physical sign that puberty has started. Her figure will start changing and she will develop hips and a waistline. She may develop quickly or slowly, as each girl's growth pattern is different. These are changes she may or may not acknowledge depending on how aware she is of her own body. At this point, it is time to start preparing her for the onset of her menses.

Preparing Your Daughter

Purchase supplies and select several different brands for your daughter to see. She may have a sensory reaction to one product and prefer another one based on criteria that do not apply to you. The color of the package, the shape of the pad, or an odor associated with the packaging will be some of her determining variables.

 Fact

Children with autism are notoriously immodest. If you permitted your kids to run around without clothing when they were young, puberty is the time to teach them modesty. Children with autism do not understand that different environments require different clothing, and you don't want your teen stripping in the grocery store.

When you begin teaching your daughter how to handle the hygiene issues of having a period, it is important that a woman be part of the instructional process. If you are a single dad, you need to find some help. A girl should never believe that it is appropriate and acceptable for any male, of any age or relationship to her, be in any kind of intimate contact with her. That is a rule that must never be broken. Single fathers can rely on their own mother, sister, a school nurse, or another trusted female. It is impossible to teach a girl what is appropriate for her own body if that rule is not adhered to closely.

Buy an easy-to-read calendar and put it in the bathroom. Begin by showing your daughter the calendar and the pads you purchased. Talk to her as though she understands each word you say even if she is totally nonverbal. Take a red pen, circle the date on the calendar, and then place some red food coloring on the pad. The goal is to imitate in a nonthreatening way what she will see when her periods begin. Handle the situation in a matter-of-fact manner. Dispose of the "used" pad, replace it with a new one, and repeat this every two to three hours. Continue this practice for about five days. Twenty-eight days later, repeat the process.

 Essential

If the menstrual cycle is extremely difficult and hygiene is a constant battle, discuss your options with your daughter's doctor. Some physicians put girls with autism on medication or give an injection to suppress their periods. This may be an option if it is medically appropriate.

When the big day arrives, and remember, you will have no warning of the actual date, fall back on your planning techniques. Keep in stride as you circle the day on the calendar and attend to hygiene. Remember to teach her proper disposal of the pads and be sure you keep a supply of her preferred brand.

There are no guarantees this will be the magic bullet and that your daughter's periods will begin and continue uneventfully. There are likely to be trying times for the entire family. Hygiene may be a continual problem or it may go smoothly, without any problems at all. Every teenage girl is different and there is no way to know how your daughter will feel about any of this. If you can convey calmness and avoid a production over the situation, the chances are greater she will take it in stride.

Birth Control

It is easier for parents to make decisions regarding their child's sexuality if they proceed thoughtfully and cautiously. Sexuality is always a matter of informed consent between two adults. Factoring in the mental age of your child and her social abilities is essential. Unfortunately, no policy can exclude the possibility of sexual conduct that is unplanned, and for girls on the autism spectrum, this is a problem.

Most states do not allow permanent methods of birth control to be used on children, even if they are over the age of majority. There are no exceptions to those laws for children with disabilities. If your child is impaired enough that having children is out of the question, check with a gynecologist and the laws in your state to find out what can and cannot be done.

So how do parents prevent an unplanned pregnancy that is the result of their child engaging in sexual contact without understanding the implications of the activity? Many physicians will prescribe a birth control method for girls with autism or other spectrum disorders that can be taken daily in a pill form, injected every few weeks (frequency depending on the patient), or implanted. The advantage to the injections or implants is that the concern is removed without the daily use of a pill. The disadvantage can be the possible side effects of these methods of birth control, including weight gain, headaches, and problems that may be associated with long-term use of these medications.

It may be unfair that parents of boys with autism do not have as much to be concerned about in this area, but the reality is that girls are at a much higher risk for the consequences of sexual activity. It is not necessary to make a point at this time regarding the responsibility of sexual behavior; the important issue is to protect your daughter.

Inappropriate Behaviors

Although there are many behaviors that can be considered inappropriate, none upset people quite like those behaviors that are sexual in nature. Because of inappropriate behaviors, the deficit in social skills is even more evident and isolating for the person with autism. Children become aware at very young ages that it is inappropriate to touch other people in certain places; a child with autism does not have that built in control and if curious may reach out to touch someone else's body. This is particularly common with adolescent boys who may try to touch a woman's breast. It is important to deal with these behaviors when a child is young so that they are not a problem when he becomes an adult.

Self-Stimulating Behaviors

This is a difficult subject for parents of kids with autism. When they discover their child actively masturbating without any discretion, they wonder how to handle the situation. To keep a proper perspective, remember almost all children masturbate. Children with autism have no inhibitions, because they are unaware of the social taboo against masturbating in public.

 Alert

If your child masturbates excessively, genital irritation can result. Be sure there is not a vaginal discharge in girls or pinworms in little children. Both can cause itchiness and irritation. An examination by your child's physician should let you know if this is a problem. Some medications used for autism, notably SSRIs (Selective Serotonin Reuptake Inhibitor), slow the libido and may be appropriate.

The mistake that parents often make—and it is an easy one to make—is to stop the behavior when they find their child masturbating in a public area. They will usually shout or sharply pull their child's hand away. That does stop the behavior, but it sends a message that sexuality and the human body are bad or dirty.

Your goal should not be to stop the behavior, but rather to redirect it to an appropriate time and location. Masturbating in the middle of the living room is not appropriate, and redirecting your child to his or her bedroom with a closed door will solve most public displays. Keep in mind that people with autism are dictated by the structure of their routine. If they are taught that their bedroom is the only acceptable location for self-stimulating behavior, they will adhere to that routine.

Inappropriate Touching of Others

The majority of paraprofessionals that work with students with autism are female. Women are also still in a majority as caregivers, whether it be at home, day care, or in other environments that care for children. A young boy with autism who has raging hormones in his system may not understand that touching others in a sexual manner is not acceptable. Do not be surprised if you find out that your son has tried this.

The behavior is not malicious or intended to degrade. Your child has no idea that it is unacceptable to touch another person inappropriately. Nevertheless, the behavior must be stopped. Although you may be able to dismiss it in a ten-year-old child, if it's allowed to continue, it will be much harder to dismiss the behavior in a thirty-year-old man.

Generally, the situation will resolve itself. A girl is less inclined to engage in this behavior, and when a boy crosses the line, a woman's natural reaction will be a slap or loud rebuke. The most important thing that parents and school personnel can do is teach your child that inappropriate touching of others is not allowed in any circumstance. It is much easier to modify behaviors in a child or teenager than it is to change the same behaviors in an adult.

There are books for young children that have drawings geared toward those who might not understand the language. The goal is to help your child with autism learn to control his sexual behavior in a way that will keep him safe.

CHAPTER 14

Life as an ASD Adult

When people begin having children, they have expectations and goals for their lives and their children's lives. One of those goals is watching a child grow to independence. Parents are truly satisfied when they know their adult child is equipped to face and handle the world. But having a child with autism causes parents to re-evaluate that goal and determine what the future will hold when their child becomes an adult.

Living Independently

In a perfect world, children with autism would mature and acquire enough skills to live on their own. They would understand the things that are needed to live safely: turning off stoves, locking doors, and handling all the daily activities about which most people never give a second thought.

 Fact

Coping depends on the ability to understand what is needed in a particular situation and being able to perform or think through what steps need to be taken. If a young person is upset or overwhelmed she might not be able to handle living independently.

Activities of Daily Living (ADL)

Before the bigger issues of independent living can be addressed, parents and caretakers must be sure that a young adult with autism can be responsible for her own personal care and hygiene. A young adult must be able to:

- Bathe or shower daily
- Independently use the bathroom
- Use deodorant, skin care products, and other toiletries appropriately
- Brush and floss her teeth
- Brush her hair
- Dress properly for weather conditions
- Dress appropriately for work, leisure, and sleep
- Determine which clothes need to be laundered
- Take medications at the proper times in the proper dosages

Most children with autism do learn all of these things and develop a routine they faithfully maintain. If you have a child who is ten years old and has not mastered some of these skills, don't worry. She may be behind, but the odds are that she will catch up and have her own system to care for herself. Parents sometimes forget that children who do not have autism resist brushing their teeth and washing their hands, so it isn't always autism that is the culprit. Sometimes it is just being a kid.

Building the Daily Care Habits

As parents work with a child to build the habits and skills she will need as an adult, they learn that her preference for living by a routine can work in their favor. If your child relies heavily on a routine to make sense of her world, use that to teach her the skills she needs.

Making Lists

Before you begin building a routine to teach activities of daily living, sit down with a piece of paper and pencil and outline all of the skills that are necessary for your child. All people have some common activities, such as bathing and using the bathroom, but there are many individual ones as well. For example, some children need to use certain skin care products to treat acne or eczema.

Make a list and divide it into three parts: morning, afternoon, and evening. In your three-part schedule, list the activities that occur, or should occur, during those times. For instance, the morning list might include using the bathroom, brushing teeth, showering, medications, and so forth. Make this list for each of the three parts of the day in your child's schedule, itemizing all the activities you can think of. Keep the list handy for a few days and add in the things you overlooked so the list will be as complete as possible.

Creating a Communication Board

Now you can start teaching your child to make this list second nature. If your child is nonverbal, make a communication board and put it in the bathroom where she will be able to reference it easily; above a sink is a good location for something of this nature. You can attach small drawings that represent the activity or you can use photographs. Attach them with Velcro so you can adjust the order in which things are done if necessary.

 Fact

An instant camera can make quick work of creating visual cues to help your child understand her life and routine. Take photos of her brushing her teeth, bathing, her clothes, and other items she uses. This will make your communication board unique and specific to her needs.

The next step is simple. Start the routine each morning with your child. Explain to her as you go through the activities what she is to do and point to the picture on the communication board. If she can understand what she reads, another option is to have a chart on the wall where she can read the activities she needs to complete. After three to four weeks, she will have developed a new routine. Keep an eye on it until you are confident she has mastered the skills. That is one less thing for you to worry about as your child learns to get herself ready each morning!

Repeat this entire procedure for the afternoon and evening care. The most important part is following the schedule closely. Be certain your child follows it as well. As mentioned before, people with autism are ruled by their routine, and this self-care routine will be something that will help your child achieve independence.

Residential Living

Many parents have their child with autism live at home after reaching adulthood. However, this is not always the best choice for an adult child or for the parents. There are other available options and there is no single, best solution for a given child. It isn't just the child's abilities that determine what is best for the family. It is also the family's needs, lifestyle, available emotional and physical resources, and finances.

Remaining at Home

This is one of the most frequently discussed topics in support groups across the country. Someone will usually, and tentatively, ask the question, "What do I do when my child is grown?" The most important consideration in deciding where your child will live as an adult should be whether the environment is productive and interesting. Whether your child lives at home with you, lives in a group home, or needs to be institutionalized, the life he leads must be actively in touch with the world around him. As a child turns into a young adult, and then from a young adult into a mature adult, his happiness and satisfaction will hinge on his environment.

One of the most distinctive aspects of autism, the tendency for introversion, makes it imperative that an adult with autism has an environment full of variety and interest. It is too easy for many people with autism to withdraw into their own world and if that is allowed to continue, they can retreat further and further from those around them. Couple that with the lack of conceptual understanding, and it is easy to see how someone with autism becomes a couch potato, staring at a television for hours on end.

If you wish to keep your adult child at home with you, be sure you have the physical and mental capacity to keep him busy. He will need to participate in various activities, have a schedule that keeps him interested, and stick to the schedule as much as possible. He will also need to be physically active. You will need to either keep up with that schedule yourself or have someone in the home who can. You will also need to plan ahead to make arrangements for someone to care for your child when age and health make it impossible for you to do so.

Group Homes

Group homes and assisted living are the options most parents choose for their children on the autism spectrum. Group homes generally have four to six residents. Two staff members are on the schedule at all times except during sleeping hours, when one is sufficient, and other personnel for special therapies come in and out. These homes are usually single-family residences in neighborhoods around the country. Group homes are very popular for several reasons:

- People with autism see others without disabilities and thus have role models outside their immediate family members.
- People in the community are exposed to autism and learn they are people like anyone else.

- Group homes with several people give everyone a chance to continue a degree of socialization.
- Therapies and education are provided to the residents in group homes and life skills are taught by staff members or other qualified people.
- Activities are planned regularly such as swimming, bowling, and field trips that everyone enjoys.
- Group homes may be permanent but they can also teach a young adult with autism the skills necessary to live independently or return home to live with parents and other family members.

Assisted living is for people with high-functioning autism who need less supervision than those in a group home. Two people may share living arrangements and have a social services worker visit daily to be sure that their needs are being met. Each of these situations would vary depending on the people involved and their abilities.

Institutionalized Living

When you think of institutions, you may think of the horror stories that you've heard rumors about or seen in films. It is true that in the past, institutions were the last stop for people with mental disabilities. It is also true that abuse and neglect were common problems for the people unfortunate enough to find themselves placed in an institution. Much of the problem came from a lack of understanding of the various disabilities and illnesses that affected people. The social isolation of an institution only added to the situation, as no one in a community really knew what was going on behind those closed doors.

Institutions in the modern era differ vastly from the creaky, ancient fortresses that were once common. Many are modern and have a homelike setting. They are clean without looking like a hospital and are geared toward meeting the needs of the residents.

They tend to be staffed by professionals who enjoy working with the mentally challenged. Yes, some of these facilities do exist.

 Essential

> Whether a parent chooses an institution, group or assisted-living, or keeps an adult child with autism at home, is a very individual choice. Don't let family, friends, or society make you feel badly about your decision. Many factors enter into the living situation of an adult child. You might seek professional advice from a counselor to consider various issues.

An institution may be appropriate for a person with autism who has behavioral disorders that can be a source of danger to him or others. Group homes or assisted-living facilities do not have the close supervision that may be necessary for such a person. Patients who have other physical complications requiring a great deal of therapy or medications may also be best suited for an institution.

Providing After You Are Gone

If you do not have a will, put down this book and call an attorney to have one drawn up immediately. After you have scheduled an appointment, make some notes about what you want to include in the will. The worst thing that could possibly happen is for something to happen to you or your spouse when you have made no provisions for your child. Everyone asks what the worst-case scenario is when you have a child with autism. It is the death of parents who have not prepared for their child.

Asset Protection
When a young couple marries and begins to build a life, they usually make plans for the future. Seldom do they think that the

decisions they make in their twenties may affect their baby when she is a senior citizen. But it is important for parents of a child with autism to protect all of their assets to provide for their child when she is an adult.

In our highly mobile society, the average family moves every seven years. Many families move more often. Most of these families own a home and as the years go by, they sell, buy, and upgrade a little each time. They start with a small home, move to a moderately sized one, and have the goal of a certain kind of house that will be their last home purchase. As a result, there is no "family home" and no mortgage ever gets paid in full.

 Alert

> If you name someone in your will to care for your child's finances, be absolutely certain of your confidence and trust in this person. It might be wise to consider a certified accountant to protect your child's interests. You also need to be sure the individual knows of your decision.

If you have not yet bought a home, it would be wise to start working toward that goal. If you stay in that house, perhaps improving or remodeling it, its value should increase as the economy improves, your mortgage payments will be relatively stable, and it will hopefully be paid in full in fifteen to thirty years. That is the most valuable asset your child could ever have. Although he would need someone to handle his finances, that house you are considering buying now, or may already own, could provide him with security for his entire life.

Cars, jewelry, paintings, stocks and bonds, and just about every other asset can go down in value. A house, on land that you own, is valuable security not only for you and your family now, but also in the distant future for your child with autism.

Trust Funds

A parent often sets up a trust fund to provide for a child's needs. Because a child with autism is not likely to understand money management when she is an adult, preparations to protect her future are important. Although a will does declare where you wish your assets to go, a trust fund has funds and assets that can be distributed over a person's lifetime. As with guardianship, it is important to select a trusted friend or organization to oversee the trust fund. It is possible to select more than one trustee if you wish to have the responsibility shared.

Each state has different laws governing how trusts are set up and maintained, and it is important that you are aware of your state's regulations. Most states have two types of trust funds, one of which is of particular interest to the parents of a child who is disabled. An after-death trust is set up to protect the financial needs of a child when both parents are deceased. An estate attorney can best advise you concerning your specific needs, concerns, and state laws.

 Essential

Although many states have made it legal for you to write your own will, this is not wise if your child has a disability. If a parent has made his own will, it is more vulnerable to being successfully contested. It would be wise to get the assistance of a licensed estate attorney.

The trustee or person you appoint to oversee the trust must be someone you trust implicitly. Trustees are held to a high accountability, both legally and morally, and although they may be paid a small fee for their services, the judgment they provide is invaluable. If you choose a family member or friend, be certain she understands financial management. If the individual can be trusted to fulfill your wishes and your child's needs, but lacks some knowledge in the finer points of money management, don't hesitate to also appoint an accountant or other professional to advise your primary trustee.

Guardians

If something happens to you or your spouse, do you know who will take care of your children—especially your child with autism? Most people feel confident that a family member would step in, but when a crisis such as this happens, it doesn't always work out that smoothly. It may be impossible for grandparents, due to age or health, to assume the responsibility for your child. It may also be more than another family member can handle if he is raising a family already. Do not assume anything.

A Serious Discussion

In choosing potential guardians, make a list of the people you feel would be best able to raise your child in the event you are unable to do so. Then talk to those people in a setting where you have their total attention. This is a serious decision for all parties concerned, and not the subject for an "off the cuff" conversation. Outline what your child's needs are now and what those needs are apt to be in the future. Explain what financial resources would be available, what health issues your child has, and what your expectations are for his future.

As you compile this list of people, think about your child, his life, and the lives of the people you are considering asking. If it is a family member, perhaps your own sister, does she have a career that might make this responsibility difficult? A career military officer may be stationed anywhere in the world or called to active service with little advance notice, and she would then have the same problem of deciding who would step in. Also, consider the person's lifestyle and how she feels about her family life. One person who has eight children might easily handle another one, even one with autism, but another person with a large family might panic at the idea of another child.

 Fact

> You may hope your other children would step in to care for their brother with autism if the need arose. But the truth is that siblings may not feel up to taking on such a challenge. It can also place an unfair burden on a sibling. If a sibling is named as a caretaker in your will, he should always agree to be named, in addition to alternate individuals.

When you approach a person about assuming care of your child, he may have several reactions. It's possible that he would want, or insist, on caring for your child. Alternatively, the person might like to think it through and consider different options. Or, he may realize immediately that this would not be the right decision for him or his family. There is no right or wrong answer to this request. Your big sister who always bailed you out of a problem may have family issues of which you are unaware that make this responsibility impossible. Your parents may have health concerns of their own that would prevent them from taking on this responsibility, even though they may wish they could step in. Your other children may be unable or unwilling to take on this responsibility.

A Controversial Choice

Sometimes parents make decisions about guardianship that are not understood by family members, and can cause conflict. It would be so easy to say that the only way to avoid a problem is not to tell anyone, reasoning that a conflict probably won't arise, but if one does, you won't have to hear about it anyway. Consider, though, the people you have chosen. If your family members do not know in advance what your wishes are, and yet you have made those choices official in your will, bad feelings could result, and a custody battle could ensue.

Many parents decide not to choose a family member to assume the custody of their child in the event it is needed.

 Essential

> Expect that you will have to revise your choice of a guardian every few years. Your child's needs will change over time and you will understand them better as he matures. Other people's lives change as well. Plan ahead and be flexible to change when it is necessary.

It may be because of a lack of closeness with other family members. Or you may know about financial or other circumstances that would limit your relatives' ability to accept this challenge. Whatever your reason, should you choose a nonrelative to care for your child in the event of your death, do not feel guilty or pressured to change your arrangements. You and your spouse, or if you are single, you alone, know what is best.

 Alert

> When you are writing your will it is also be important to include a Living Will. This states your wishes about what you want done in case of a serious hospitalization or accident. It would be tragic to have most of your money go to pay for a prolonged hospitalization or a long-term care facility.

When you have a list of people who would be willing to act as guardian, state those people by name in your will as your choices to raise your children. It is wise to have several names in case something prevents one of them from stepping in. If you have more than one name on the list in your will, you can avoid having to rewrite it every six months or so, and it will save attorney's fees. It will also give you peace of mind to know that you have done all you can to protect your child and his interests.

Financial Protection

Every family attempts to protect itself financially, but when there is a child with autism involved, this protection becomes much more critical. Mom and dad find they are making decisions that affect the "here and now," as well as the distant future.

Insurance

When you are young, you think you will live forever. Everyone realizes her own mortality at a different age, but it doesn't usually happen when a person is in her twenties. However, that is the time when life insurance is less inexpensive and easy to acquire.

A staggering number of parents find themselves widowed with small children, and out of those, a large number of them have no life insurance to fall back on. Imagine a woman who has lost her husband very unexpectedly who has been staying at home with the kids and has no financial resources available. It is as scary as it sounds. Social Security will pick up the burden for a time. for the children, and you may qualify for Supplemental Security Insurance or another form of state aid, but these are not long-term solutions.

One of the smartest investments you can make when you have children, especially if a child is disabled, is to purchase as much life insurance as you can afford. When you are young and healthy, the rates are much lower than if you wait until your late thirties or forties to purchase a policy.

IRAs and Other Funds

Parents can, through their employer, set up various financial plans that should protect and increase their money over the years. IRAs and other retirement plans may be able to protect a family in different ways. Tax benefits can be seen immediately, and funds will be available to provide for family members upon retirement or in the case of an unexpected death. IRAs supersede the will, so be certain you keep your beneficiary or beneficiaries updated.

Every state differs in regulations regarding financial matters. Financial planning is a complex subject with many pitfalls for the uninformed. If you are planning to set up a portfolio for your family's security, consult with an accountant and estate-planning attorney for the best course of action. You will be preparing not just for your lifetime, but for your child's lifetime as well.

CHAPTER 15

Assistive Techniques and Technologies

A ny device or item that can help a person with autism compensate for his or her deficits is considered assistive. There are many forms of assistive devices—some are based on sophisticated technology and others are very basic and can be made at home. Anything you use or adapt that helps your child function to the best of his ability is an assistive device.

A Mind Like a Computer

The 1990s saw many significant changes beyond just the dramatic increase in autism. It also was the time of technological breakthroughs; once previously inaccessible, computers moved from the scientific world into the average American home. Home computers became as common as microwave ovens. And for children with autism, computers have become tools to increase understanding, reduce undesirable behaviors, and learn to become more independent in an adult world.

Children with autism seem to have a natural flair for computers. It takes little time for them to understand how the computer operates. Their abilities on the computer are often amazing; a child may be nonverbal and restricted by his own repetitive activities, but put that child in front of a computer and you are the one limited, not him. Most children with autism have the ability to understand computers better than they understand other human beings.

 Fact

> If your child engages in self-stimulating and obsessive repetitive behaviors, consider getting him a computer. It does not have to be a top-of-the-line model; a basic computer on which you can install programs and run CD-ROMs will be sufficient. The unacceptable behaviors will likely be reduced, and he will be learning simultaneously.

Visual "Thinking"

Visualization is a very helpful tool for people with autism. The autistic mind processes things visually, so it is the strongest learning center for a person with autism. Think of the mind and its functions as being similar to a series of snapshots. Each photograph represents a memory or an understanding of something specific. The brain of a person with autism stores memories and knowledge in that format. One snapshot or picture of something tells him what he needs to know.

Instead of being linear, visual thinking is associative. The memories and knowledge of a person with ASD are not filed in the brain the same way that they are in a person without autism.

Computers also "think" in that manner. Each file or "memory" can be brought up on the screen, intact and self-contained. If you can access that file, you can access everything you need to know about that memory. And carrying this a step further, associative links, tying together different parts of the computer, create the complete memory. Therefore, seemingly unrelated memories are linked together to make a whole picture. The computer sees the link and understands why, even if the typical person does not.

You can turn off the sound on a computer and it will still work. You may not understand why it works the way it does at times, but it is unrelenting in its way of doing things. In order to use a computer, you must adapt to it; the computer will never change. A person with autism thinks in a similar manner, and what seems like techno-babble is in fact a logically ordered visual system used by both the autistic mind and the computer. Computers and people with autism think alike.

Using Computers for Your Child's Benefit

Many people reserve the use of the home computer as a reward for children who have successfully completed their chores or homework. It is viewed as a recreational item, and like any privilege, it can be removed. But for a child with autism, a computer is an important part of everyday life and not just a privilege; it is a communication tool, learning aid, and social companion. Because of this, when you integrate a computer into the everyday life of your child with autism, it should be viewed as a necessity and not a luxury.

 Question

Is there aid available to help my child get a computer?
It is acceptable to use SSI money to purchase a computer and programs for your child because it is considered an assistive device. You just need to be able to show that the computer is for your child's needs and that it is not the family computer.

If a child needs a computer at school, this should be written into the IEP. Some states have special funds to buy these for children in special education who need them.

The IEP should also include the amount of time and number of days a computer is to be used by your child. Parents need to monitor that this occurs because sometimes a computer will sit in a closet and not be used. School districts have computer consultants or can hire them and they can help with the choice of the right computer and software. You may need to request this in your child's IEP.

Children who have autism have realized many benefits from their use of computers. Attention, motivation, and organizational skills have increased from computer usage, and children show more independent behaviors and greater self-reliance. Socialization has also improved, and expressive language becomes more appropriate and useful for a child with autism. The computer can help to put your child's disordered world in order.

Hardware That Helps

Computer accessories can help children with autism learn various programs, games, and activities. For children with deficits in fine motor skills, some of these devices can make the computer easier to use. Other devices can help a child who struggles with the understanding of concepts to bridge the gap between the abstract and the concrete.

 Fact

A QWERTY keyboard has the keys placed in the traditional arrangement, with the first letters in the top row spelling out the word "QWERTY." This keyboard is usually not difficult for a child to learn. ABC keyboards are also available, but these may or may not be suitable for your child. But if your child is having difficulty with a keyboard or other computer hardware, there are many adaptations that a consultant can suggest, so it is important that their services be requested and written into the IEP.

Monitor Devices

One of the most popular assistive devices on the market is the touch screen window. This allows a person to use the computer with limited or no need for a mouse. Schools and libraries often have a touch screen window because it reduces the risk of a mouse being lost or stolen, so if your child is older, she may have already used this device.

A touch screen is a major benefit for children who have a conceptual problem understanding that the mouse controls movement on the screen. When a child can become involved directly with the computer, she will derive many more benefits from its possibilities. Removing the mouse for a child that struggles with this issue will reduce frustration and the subsequent behaviors that may occur.

If your child has problems with overstimulation when using a computer, it could be caused by glare from the computer. Some people are ultrasensitive to the light of a computer monitor, which can cause fatigue, eyestrain, and headaches. Many inexpensive filters are available that can be placed over the screen to reduce the glare and make the time on the computer less fatiguing. This will also ease overstimulation, if that is a concern.

Keyboard Devices

Some children with autism have problems with fine motor skills and have limited dexterity. An alternative keyboard can ease the problems encountered when attempting to type on the small standard-size keys. This is also good for preschool-age children who are learning hand-eye coordination.

When shopping for alternative keyboards, remember that you won't be able to find every feature on one keyboard. You need to prioritize your child's needs and then make a decision. If she has dexterity issues, a keyboard with large keys would be helpful. If she has vision problems, a lighted keyboard would help. There are many sizes and shapes of keyboards; comparing what is available will help you make the best choice. An assistive technology consultant or those at the nation-wide Alliance for Technology Access centers should be able to help you make the best decision. The National Technical Assistance Center has a website at *www.taalliance.org.*

After the computer is set up, if your child has some problems with the operation of the keyboard, check in the operating system for accessibility options. You can program the keyboard for specialized functions—for example, to ignore rapidly repeating keystrokes if your child tends to rest her hands directly on the keys. Several options can personalize the computer and make it easier for your child to operate.

Mouse Devices

The computer you bought probably came with a mouse that was the most basic model available. It left-clicks, right-clicks, and moves the cursor. It is small and probably not very efficient. Other options may work better for your child.

 Alert

When choosing the peripheral equipment for your child's computer, cross off wireless mouse from your shopping list. There are few things more upsetting than an enraged child with autism who can't find his computer mouse. A corded mouse is more difficult to throw in an anger outburst.

Trackball mice are very popular, and with good reason. The mouse is stationary, solid, and versatile. The ball is in a fixed position within the mouse and is operated by either fingers or thumb. Left- and right-handed versions are available. The trackball is easy to get used to and will give your child more control of activities on the computer.

Useful Software

Once your child's computer is set up, it is time to load it with programs and software. A trip to your local computer store will probably result in your finding more programs than your child could ever use. The trick is to find the programs that will be most helpful and won't be a waste of time and money.

Look for programs that are educational but are also fun. No one can expect any child to stick with a program if it is boring and lifeless. Math programs based on popular cartoon characters are a great favorite and illustrate clearly the concepts necessary to understand the skills being taught in the program. Instead of just hearing that one plus one equals two, a computer program can show it. This will be helpful to the primary learning method of your child—the more visual the program, the better it will work for him.

 Essential

Many online sources sell computer software programs at reduced prices. Compare the prices before you purchase anything. If you are unfamiliar with a site, check its privacy and security policies; order one product, and if you are satisfied with the service, you can go back for future purchases.

Programs created specifically for the child with ASD will be extremely useful but a little more difficult to find. Buying these programs online is the most convenient method. These programs can address the problems children on the autism spectrum face regularly; speech (receptive and expressive), dexterity, and social interaction are some of the areas these programs address.

Texting and Other Mobile Communications

Because a child with autism often is unusually gifted in the use of a computer, she might also be able to handle other forms of communications. This would be a very individual way of communicating and would have to be carefully controlled. In general, handheld communication devices can be a real problem. They also can be easily lost, so they are probably not the best idea except in special cases. Since impulse control can be a problem, that is another consideration. Socialization should be encouraged in different activities with other kids, not by the use of a cell phone or texting.

Service Dogs

The use of service dogs or other animals for assistance is a relatively new concept for people with autism. Dogs are the most commonly used animals and are worth considering for your child. A service dog can reduce the risk of elopement, aid in socialization, and protect in a public environment. If that sounds like your own private police department and hospitality host rolled into one, you're right. It is!

 Alert

The Canine Companions for Independence organization has centers across the United States. Their website is *www.cci.org*. If your child is accepted for their program a family member must spend two weeks training with the child. Your child should be the only one allowed to handle or play with the dog. Others should be asked not to pet the dog.

Before you get so enthusiastic that you run down to the local dog adoption center, several things must be considered. Anytime an animal is brought into your home, whether it is trained by an agency or you train it yourself, it is a decision that must be weighed carefully. Remember that a service dog is there to work, and work he will; whenever your child and his service dog are together, the dog is working. But a dog is still a dog; it has to be allowed to play, dig holes, torment the family cat, and do all the things dogs do. Your success will be determined by how well you integrate the needs of the child and the needs of the dog.

Family Considerations

It is vitally important that a child not be frightened of large dogs before you get a service dog. If your child is very young and you are considering this option for the future, expose your child to larger dogs that you know are comfortable with children. It can be alarming for a child who has never been around a large dog to suddenly have an animal at eye level. A hesitant or scared child will not bond with the dog, and no training in the world will allow them to perform as a good team.

 Fact

> When a child approaches a dog, he usually has open arms, totally unrestrained behavior, and tends to try to pet or hug the dog. A child will understand better how to interact with a dog if he has been raised with one. If you are considering having a service dog in the future, it could help to have a pet dog now.

One parent must be involved in the dog/child team. If there are many caretakers involved, this will be confusing for both the child and the dog. One adult who can supervise the team and provide the dog with direction, showing it what is expected at a given moment will help the dog perform to the best of its ability. Children best adapt to a service dog after they become toddlers and before they enter school for the first time. Although there are exceptions, of course, a child between the ages of two or three and six will be more receptive to the concept of dog/child teamwork. Also, pets are fun for kids and teach responsibility in caring for something other than themselves.

Canine Considerations

Dogs are still dogs, regardless of their occupation. It is important that a fenced yard be available for the dog so it can go outside for play and relaxation. Think of this dog as an employee as well as a family member and service animal. Everyone needs off-hours, and a service dog is no exception to this. Even the best-trained service dog is not above treeing a cat, burying a bone, or rolling in the mud. These activities also provide exercise that is essential to the physical and mental health of the dog.

 Essential

The Department of Justice states that animals other than dogs may be used as a service animal. Cats, ferrets, and parrots are very helpful service animals with a child who has autism. With all pets, there are precautions to take; animals should never be kissed around the mouth and children must always wash their hands after handling a pet. Cat scratch fever can cause a serious infection and will need medical treatment.

Like any other animal, dogs can become ill or need preventative medical attention. Veterinary bills can be expensive. It is wise to have a bank account set up that you put funds into on a monthly basis to cover any expensive procedures or treatments that may be needed. Emergencies happen as well, and having that backup fund is akin to medical insurance for the dog.

Different breeds of dog require different grooming. A dog with a fuller coat will need frequent brushing to stay neat. Some children are interested in this, whereas others are not able or willing to perform this task. Of course, you can brush a dog regularly if you are willing to give the time required. Remember that nail clipping, dental care, and other grooming needs specific to a particular breed should be taken into account when a dog is being selected.

Different dogs have different dietary needs. Some dogs cannot tolerate certain foods, and high-grade dog foods are the best for a dog that is working full-time with a child. A working dog should not be allowed to become obese, and a child should be taught not to feed the dog table scraps.

Other Assistive Devices

You do not need a technological piece of equipment to provide an assistive device to your child. Many of the most efficient items are readily available at any variety store. If you think of a step stool as an assistive device for someone who can't reach the top of the refrigerator, it is easy to understand how many things can be used to help your child compensate.

Next time you visit your local variety or office supply store, take a shopping cart and load it with things you think could be useful in helping your child. Some ideas to get you started are provided, but use your imagination:

- Dry erase boards, either formatted for scheduling or blank, or possibly both
- Inexpensive photo albums
- Notebook rings that come loose in a package
- Plastic storage bins of varying sizes
- Sidewalk chalk in various colors
- Yarn or string
- Magnetic letters and numbers
- Pens and pencils personalized with your child's name
- A laminator

Consider your child's strengths and weaknesses and be a little creative in coming up with solutions. For example, small storage bins could hold laminated cards that show an activity or chore that has to be done. This would help a child who does not sequence daily activities well. As your child completes each activity—such as brushing his teeth—he can move the card to the "Job Completed" bin. This will assist with sequencing and will provide motivation because the task completion is easily seen.

Sidewalk chalk can be used to provide direction if a child tends to wander when she goes outside with you; it can also show the limits of an area she is allowed to explore. Personalized writing tools are a great way to teach ownership; if your child uses the entire family's belongings, having her name on things will help her understand what is hers and what isn't. You do have to be careful that a child's name is not on something visible to a stranger. If it is, a stranger can call a child by name and perhaps lure the child away. Magnetic letters and numbers can be used in many ways—to mark a special occasion or holiday or to put up a goal for the day. You are limited only by your imagination.

Toys as Learning Tools

All toys can be considered assistive devices and learning tools if you consider what a child's job is, and the purpose of a toy. A child's job is to play; through playing, a child learns to maneuver successfully in the world as he matures. Toys are his tools and equipment, and sometimes they are even his teachers. Every toy has something within it that teaches a child.

Finding toys that assist is not very difficult. What can be difficult is figuring out, as an adult, how a toy can help. Expanding your definition of what assistive means will help you think "outside the box" and see the potential in many different toys. Toys will not provide direct assistance for a particular task at a given moment.

But they are still assistive because of the manner in which they aid a child to function in an area in which he is deficient.

Although it is important to educate and assist a child as he is growing, it is also important not to overwhelm him. Too much therapy, too many exercises, and not enough time to just "hang out" are difficult for a child. Parents tend to worry if they are not enriching their child's mind every waking second, but the reality is that constant activity will only create stress. Children with autism have enough stress trying to cope with a world that makes little sense to them.

A child can be outside playing with dirt and water and, upon discovering that together they make mud, has learned something. If nothing else, the child has learned that small quantities of water can be a wonderful thing! Yes, they are entertained, but by its very nature, life is a continually unfolding learning process that does not cease.

If you see a toy that really isn't an educational toy, but you know your child would love it, buy it. Let him enjoy it. No one goes to work (play for the child) without a break every so often. The day is full of activities to challenge and energize your child; sometimes it would be nice to just kick back with a teddy bear.

CHAPTER 16

Challenging Obstacles

Having to deal with autism on a daily basis seems like challenge enough. However, every problem, hidden or obvious, is an opportunity for a developmental step to be taken. Approach each day as though victories are waiting to be made, and the problems will be less daunting. A problem is merely a solution in disguise and may take some creative thinking to resolve.

Communicating Needs

One of the most important things you can do for your child is to meet her needs. Many times, however, children with autism have trouble expressing their needs in a way you can understand. This can be frustrating for you as well as for your child. It is a waste of time and very discouraging for everyone if you continue to offer one thing and then another to help your child, only to be rejected.

The Frustration of the ASD Child

Frustration for a child with autism is a terrible thing. It can lead to impatience, irritability, anger, and tantrums. Meltdowns can occur and the child can become completely out of control. Remember how you felt the last time you were frustrated about something? Your child feels the same way but lacks the communication to express it and the maturity to understand that it is temporary.

Chapter 6 provided valuable information regarding frustration resulting in tantrums and meltdowns. Frustration can also betray its presence in other ways. Although anger is the most common manifestation of frustration, some children withdraw and display their frustration quietly. These children may begin an extreme display of repetitive behavior, such as rocking or head banging. Some children will shake all over or bite themselves on the arm. You can almost hear them shouting from deep inside, "Will you please figure out what I need!"

 Essential

When a child is upset, parents want to reach out to the child. Because autism creates a sensory system that is always on red alert, hugs and love may be met with resistance. This is not a sign of bad parenting, so do not let yourself feel badly if your child does not want to be touched when she is upset.

Telepathy Would Help!

Every mother and father of a child with autism will tell you that they would give anything to get into their child's head for a few hours. How the thought processes of an autistic mind work is not well understood. There are some documented papers and books written by people who have "come out" of autism to report what they experienced as a child. But it is doubtful that reading about those emotions and experiences is anything like actually experiencing them.

Until you can take a pill to read minds, you are going to have to attempt to anticipate what it is your child needs. Bottom line: You are going to have to guess. Most children with autism will try to communicate what they want, so as long as you can continue the effort to help him, you can avert a tantrum. Giving up will only anger him more, so don't get so frustrated yourself that you give up. If you are using a communication board, you will be much better off, as your child will have a place to start his efforts at communication.

If your child is still learning how to communicate, just do the best you can; don't beat yourself up over the situation, and don't think you are a bad parent, because you aren't. Parenting is a creative experience. There is not a book written that could tell you everything you need to know to care for your own child. There are needs unique to her that you will discover as you wing it through this part of your life. This is true for all children, those with and without autism.

 Alert

When a child is unable to communicate her needs, she is just as frustrated as you are. Communication works both ways and parents just want to understand. Try to step back for a moment, look at the scene objectively, and imagine what your child may be thinking. She wants to communicate as much as you do.

Illness

"I couldn't believe it. I didn't get him to the doctor for two days. I didn't even know he was sick." A mother spoke with all the guilt she was feeling. "I should have known. I don't think I am a very good mom." This mom didn't realize that there was no way she could have known her child was ill. Contrary to what children think, parents do not have eyes in the back of their heads and are not able to read minds.

Objective and Subjective Symptoms

Some symptoms are obvious. A child who is vomiting is clearly ill and needs attention. You won't know exactly what the child feels, but you will see that he is sick and needs immediate treatment. Likewise, a rash can be seen and treated. These are objective symptoms, which means they can be measured, seen, heard, or felt by another person.

A subjective symptom, on the other hand, is a symptom that the patient perceives and experiences. A rash, felt subjectively by the patient, is experienced through itching and burning. This symptom, unlike the visible spots, cannot be measured or even proven. Itching is subjective.

You will have little trouble spotting the objective symptoms, and as time passes, you will get better and better at this. You will develop a sixth sense that will alert you that your child is ill—long before a parent of a child without autism might notice the same illness. The clues are subtle but you will learn to notice them and know there is a problem to be handled.

 Essential

Most children become cranky when they are ill and this characteristic is intensified if the child has autism. Since autism causes behavioral difficulties, imagine how those difficulties manifest themselves when an illness develops. How do you tell whether the behavior is worse or just manifesting differently? It is a problem for the parents in trying to determine if their child is ill.

Subjective symptoms are another matter entirely and create particular problems for parents with children who have communication difficulties. The subjective feelings of illness are often what prevent a child from getting sicker than necessary because he can tell his parents how he is feeling, and they can then start appropriate treatment at home or with a physician. A child without autism will come home from school and announce he has a headache and feels rotten. Mom or dad will feel his forehead, put him to bed to be on the safe side, and take preventative measures to keep the child from becoming sicker. It isn't that simple for your child with autism. He will come home from school with the same headache, feel just as miserable, and you won't have a clue.

This is where guilt comes in. Big time guilt! The next morning your child awakens with a fever and rash, is very lethargic, has glassy eyes, and you nominate yourself for the "worst parent in the world" award. Then it's off to the doctor and you come back home with the frustrating diagnosis of "it's a virus," and everyone moves on. You are not the worst parent in the world. Not even close.

Is My Child Sick?

It is very difficult to determine if a child with autism is ill unless the objective symptoms jump out and announce themselves. Even experienced parents will not notice the clues that indicate illness. Watch for alterations in your child's routine. You know that your child has a routine and you are quite familiar with it; your whole life is scheduled according to that routine. When it changes abruptly for no apparent reason, that is a red flag something is wrong and it is time to investigate the possibility your child is getting sick.

Behaviors are another indicator of illness. This is a bit tricky, behaviors can change; waxing and waning behaviors are typical for children with autism. For example, a child may line up objects around the house and you expect this. It may be more prevalent on one day over another, but it is something you know will happen. But if suddenly, everything in your house is lined up and your child becomes very aggressive about keeping his lines in order, this is a new manifestation of a previously observed behavior. The exaggeration of the behavior is an objective symptom; it tells you that he is possibly experiencing a subjective symptom that he has been unable to relate.

Other clues can be found in activity levels. A child who suddenly curls up on the sofa, covers himself with a blanket, and stares at the television is probably not up to snuff. How does your child react to his siblings or pets? Is it typical or does he refuse to interact in his normal manner? If your child would never turn down a tussle with a sister and he rejects her baiting him, he may be sick. If your child tends to reject physical closeness as a rule but suddenly shows a desire to be hugged and cuddled, feel his forehead while you are getting that snuggle—you may find that he has a fever. When activities that are part of the routine are ignored in favor of just lying down, you need to look into it.

 Fact

> Eating habits are another way to determine if a child is feeling ill. When a child with autism rejects his favorite foods, look for symptoms of an illness. (If his favorite food is grilled cheese sandwiches but one day he pushes them away with a look of disinterest, it is time to look a little deeper.) Do his eyes look flat or glassy? Does he rub his tummy or try to lie down? Use your instincts as a parent and check for a hot forehead or signs of a cold.

Trusting yourself isn't the easiest thing to do and it is the hardest thing to learn. But your child is tougher than you think, and if you miss a cold or flu that is beginning, both of you will be fine. As you and your child learn more and more about each other, you will be surprised how quickly you will tune into him when he isn't feeling well.

Running Away

Safety is a constant worry for the parents of a child with autism. The world seems fraught with perils that their child doesn't understand. One way to ease the worry is to establish a routine of your own. It will become part of the entire family's life, and although you will never stop feeling the concern and worry, you will know you are doing all you can to prevent an accident or tragedy.

Elopement is perhaps the single biggest cause of gray hair in parents of children with autism. Elopement, or being "a runner," means that a child has a knack for escaping her home, or other environments, such as school, and wandering off, oblivious to her surroundings. The children who elope have skills that would make Houdini envious. It seems they can unlock any lock, get through any opening, take apart any mechanism that is a barrier, and do it quietly and quickly. The world is literally theirs, and they don't hesitate to wander off in it.

If you have a child who tends to elope—and most children with autism do—take every precaution to prevent your child from escaping without your knowledge. Extra locks on doors, a service dog, or a security system are all options that can make your life easier and your child safer. Remember, windows are a handy exit point for a child bent on leaving, and they need to be secured as well.

The goal is not to prevent your child from exploring her environment. This is normal and natural and should be done with your supervision. Children with autism are oblivious to danger. That is a concept they do not grasp, and they could walk right in front of a moving car without any sense of consequences. Protection with freedom is the best way to handle a child who elopes.

A Missing Child

When children go missing, it is frightening. However, it is important to keep things in perspective. Very few children are actually abducted by strangers; these events make the news because they are relatively uncommon. Having said that, however, a child who elopes is much more likely to find himself in an environment where the risk of abduction is higher. The first step to prevent this tragedy is to prevent elopement from happening.

The second step is to be prepared if the unthinkable should happen. Keep current photographs of your child on hand, and give a set to a family member or neighbor to keep as well. Talk to your local police department and explain your child's autism so that they are aware of his disability and the potential issues. Be aware of people who enter your house for repairs and services and keep a list of their names and the companies they work for. Have a cell phone with you at all times—a parent should be able to be reached at all times, and this is especially true if your child is disabled.

 Essential

In public, do not use your child's name excessively. Children will go to an adult who knows his name almost without exception. Even if a child understands the concept of what a stranger is, that child will not consider a person who knows his name to be a stranger. Names on visible objects are also not a good idea.

Your child should be wearing an identification bracelet that has his name, address, phone number, and any important medical information printed on it. Above all, it should have "nonverbal autistic" engraved on it, if this is the case. If emergency personnel are ever involved with your child, they need to know about the deficits in his communication skills.

If a child ever goes missing, contact the police immediately. Many police departments will not institute an immediate search for an older child because they assume he is likely to be a runaway. If you have already contacted the police department to make them aware of your child's disability, you will not have to explain about autism and elopement. If they are aware of your child's autism, they can begin to assist immediately.

Safety Concerns

Most other safety issues are the same ones all parents have with young children, only amplified because of the autism. Keep in mind the disregard for danger that most children with autism have.

The following list is by no means conclusive, but it highlights some of the more important safety issues within the home:

- Stoves, refrigerators, microwave ovens, and irons are items that intrigue children and can cause serious injury.
- Electrical appliances (hair dryers, curling irons, shavers, etc.) in the bathroom are an accident waiting to happen.
- Water and a young child with autism are a dangerous combination. Be sure your child eventually learns to swim, but keep in mind how hazardous a bathtub can be. Also check the temperature of your hot water. A child can be badly scalded if the water is too hot. The hot water heater should be turned down below a temperature of 120° Fahrenheit.
- The family medications should be in a box that can be locked with a key, as an independent child may attempt to treat herself.
- Keep mirrors or glass doors out of your child's bedroom, and if a tantrum begins near glass, remove her immediately to a safer location.
- Electrical outlets are something "open" in the eyes of a child with compulsive tendencies; if she attempts to plug something into the outlet, she could be injured seriously. Special covers that are hard to remove can be purchased for outlets.

 Alert

Teach your child the sign for "help" whether or not she uses sign language. Be sure everyone she is regularly in contact with also knows the sign so they can respond to her. This one sign can make all the difference in the world and could prevent some real problems.

Many things will become second nature to you as you go throughout your day. Washing machines and dryers, for example, can be hazardous for young children and for their pets. Cats do not enjoy the spin cycle—and, yes, it does happen. Scissors and children with autism can be disastrous. Most of the things that happen will be laughed about later, but it is worth the extra work to prevent a terrible accident from occurring.

Toilet Training

Facing a major developmental milestone such as toilet training is daunting to the most experienced of parents. Both the child and the parent can end up frustrated, exhausted, and no further ahead. Remember this one tip if you remember nothing else, and repeat it like a mantra: How does my child view this situation? If everything you attempt to teach is approached from that standpoint, everything will become easier . . . a lot easier.

 Alert

> You may have to find some very creative ways to decrease your child's fear of toileting. A Walkman or iPod with favorite music could help with the fear of the toilet. Keeping a favorite book in the bathroom could give you some one-to-one reading time with your child. Talking in a soothing voice will also be helpful.

The issues of training a child who has few or no receptive skills, a lack of conceptual thinking, and no understanding of imitative behavior are unique. Your child may have additional complicating factors related to sensory problems. A child who is oversensitive to sensory stimuli may panic at the feeling of something passing from his body. A child who is insensitive may not even notice.

The Social and Language Symptoms

One of the primary symptoms of autism is the impairment in socialization skills. Children without autism will learn toilet training because they understand it will make their parents happy and they may get a reward. It is a game of give and take, and they are happy to participate. However, a child with autism may not have that kind of incentive and will be disinterested in the social gain of using the bathroom.

 Fact

Motivation is necessary to learn a new behavior. Although a child with autism is not motivated to learn through imitative behavior, he does have one powerful motivator to use: the completion of an activity. A child with autism will be very pleased at his ability to complete something.

Language difficulties complicate the transition from diaper to bathroom. When you are unable to explain what you want, how to do it, and why it should be done, you are at a disadvantage. Children who have receptive abilities may understand a portion of what you are saying, but if a child has no receptive skills, it will be much more difficult. He may even wish to please but has no idea of what is expected of him.

Sensory Problems

Most people are in tune with their own bodies. They are aware when their stomach growls, and they know when a sneeze is coming. They certainly are aware when their bladder or bowel signals the need to be emptied. Children with autism, however, may not be aware of this urgency or understand what they are to do about it.

If that weren't enough, the bathroom is a place of constant sensory stimuli. The water is running, the sounds of a fan may be heard, the toilet itself is cold, the flushing is a strange sound, and what may be the worst is that this activity requires the removal of clothing. All of those sensory triggers come rushing in all at once and if a child has problems with sensory overload, he may max out. If you have a half-bathroom in your house, consider using that for your training. There are no distracting elements that send the message of multiple uses for a bathroom. Bathtubs, hair dryers, and toothbrushes send a different message from what you are teaching right now.

The Power of Visualization

Visualization ties language, the weakest skill a person with autism has, to the strongest skill, seeing. Using visual clues is essential to toilet training your child.

If you can communicate the desired behavior, your child will be much more compliant. Nothing is worse for anyone, with or without autism, than not understanding what is expected. This is exacerbated in a child with autism with the learning of a major new skill such as using the bathroom. It is essential that the sequence of activities is clearly explained by you and understood by your child.

Visually Assisting Sequencing

A small communication board is very useful in communicating with your child. You will have something to show your child, and he will have something to reference. Simple paper with drawings or pictures that have been laminated is all that you need to create an effective system. He will see the pictures, hear your voice and the words you say, and learn what is expected of him, and when it is appropriate. The goal is to reduce the confrontation that occurs because of frustration.

A good visual sequencing communication board will have the following instructions on it:

1. Pull down pants.
2. Pull down underwear.
3. Sit on potty-chair or toilet.
4. Use toilet paper if appropriate (tailor the communication board to a boy or girl).
5. Place toilet paper in the toilet.
6. Flush toilet.
7. Pull up underwear.
8. Pull up pants.
9. Wash hands.
10. Return to normal activities.

You can tailor this list to meet your child's specific needs. Just remember you are establishing a routine. It is easier to start a routine now than it is to change one in the future. Adapt the communication board to fit your house, your routine, and your child's needs.

 Essential

Scheduling bathroom times is a good way to begin toilet training. Every hour on the hour, or every thirty minutes for some children, is a good place to start. Your child will learn that certain times on the clock mean it is that time again. Setting a kitchen timer might help you keep track of the toileting schedule.

Visual Cues

One of the most important visual aids you can use is the one indicating a child needs to use the bathroom. This visual aid is something he may use all of his life if he does not have proficient speech. The use of a visual prop for this is also helpful in setting the "tone" and notifying your child of the activity. Many people use an object such as a rubber duck; picking up the rubber duck indicates the bathroom is the next stop. Your child can also use this cue once he is older to tell you that he needs to use the bathroom.

Even better than using a prop, which can get lost or misplaced, is to use the ASL sign for "bathroom." This can't be lost, is appropriate for all ages, is discreet, and can easily be understood.

Problems and Complications

Toilet training a child rarely happens without any problems. You won't get out of this without something that baffles you. If you are unable to think of a creative way to deal with a problem, speak to your child's occupational or sensory integration therapist. Some common problems and solutions are:

- **Refusing to use the toilet at all.** Increasing fluids and fiber is helpful but if the problem is severe, talk to your child's doctor, as severe constipation can result from refusing to have a bowel movement.
- **Refusing to use toilet paper.** This is a common problem and is often due to sensory issues. Trying different brands of tissue (without scents or colors) may be a solution. Be certain it is plumbing-safe if you try a different method, such as baby wipes.
- **Using too much toilet paper.** All children are guilty of this one. Some easy solutions are counting squares, measuring it against a line on the wall, or replacing it with facial tissue.
- **Inaccurate aim.** This is something boys have a tendency to do and can be helped by using a target in the toilet. Floating something in the water can give them something to aim for. Just be sure it is safe for your plumbing. If all else fails, show him how to clean the seat with a baby wipe.

- **Flushing inappropriate items.** Do not ever let your child see you flush anything that doesn't belong there! You understand the goldfish went to fish heaven; your child may not understand that the cat shouldn't go as well.

This list is by no means complete. Your child will come up with his or her own unique difficulties and challenges. The good news is that you will come up with just as many unique solutions.

CHAPTER 17

Intervention for
ASD Children

B eginning early intervention is the most important step that
parents can take to help their child with autism. If various
therapies and treatments can begin before the age of three, the
development of a child with autism is greatly enhanced. Your
child's potential abilities will be expanded as he matures, and he
will learn to relate to others in a way that did not happen before
early intervention became the norm. Early intervention involves
physicians, therapists, and schools, as well as parents, of course.

Who's Who Among Physicians

Although everyone agrees that finding a good physician can make
all the difference to a family with a special needs child, they will
also agree that it is very difficult to find one who is familiar with
autism. A smart doctor will admit if she isn't well informed on the
topic and will refer you to a specialist, or she will make an effort to
learn all she can to benefit her patients. Throughout your child's
growing years, you will likely have contact with several different
physicians.

The Pediatrician
Pediatricians are specialists who provide the medical care of
children. They see children from birth to age eighteen and beyond

in certain circumstances. Pediatrics is a specialty of medicine, as children are not just miniature adults—their health needs and issues are different and must be treated differently from the way an adult would be treated. Pediatricians have many years of college and training: eight years of college and medical school, one year of pediatric internship, and two or more years in pediatric residency.

 Fact

A good pediatrician will take the time to learn about your entire family. She will ask about your family life and history. She is not prying but rather is attempting to understand the environment in which your child lives and how it affects his health and well-being.

A pediatrician should posses many qualities, but some of the most important for your family are a kind nature, gentleness, the ability to relate to nonverbal children, and a lot of patience. Pediatricians should be involved in keeping your child well, not just treating him when he is sick.

 Essential

If you are not comfortable with either the pediatrician or the staff and if the office doesn't seem well run and is not clean and child-friendly, it would be wise to keep looking. You may need to visit two or three pediatricians before you find just the right one.

Many parents feel that a team is necessary to provide proper care of their child, and the pediatrician is one of the most valued members of that team. The pediatrician should feel much the same way—that she is a member of a team that has been assembled to help your child. Selecting the right pediatrician, one with whom you feel comfortable, is important. Begin by speaking with family and friends and, of course, your support group; collect a list of names and organize yourself so that you find the best physician you can. Then make an initial appointment with the doctor you select to see how you and your child relate to the doctor as well as the office staff.

The Pediatric Neurologist

Neurology is the study of brain and nervous system disorders. Pediatric neurologists are specialized in both neurology and pediatrics and have training in both fields. They treat conditions from headaches to brain tumors. Some have a special interest in autism, but many do not.

A pediatric neurologist will not be the source of primary care for your child. In other words, don't call her office for a sore throat or rash. However, if your child has a coexisting condition such as a seizure disorder, you will be working closely with this physician for many years. A physician who is aggressively pursuing continuing education regarding autism would be your best choice, as information on autism changes frequently.

The Child Psychiatrist or Psychologist

It is hard not to balk when you are advised to consult with a child psychiatrist or psychologist. To keep this in the proper light, remember that mental health professionals do more than work with mental illness; they have a unique understanding of how structural brain disorders affect behavior and how best to treat those problems. There is a definite relationship between the mind, body, and spirit, and a psychologist and psychiatrist work in those somewhat nebulous areas.

A psychiatrist is a physician who has had additional training studying the brain and the mind. She will have had twelve years of training. The psychiatrist can prescribe medications, whereas other experts in mental health cannot. A child psychiatrist may also be helpful as a family adjusts to the diagnosis of autism.

Clinical psychologists will have either a master's degree or doctorate. One of their most important roles is to perform the diagnostic testing for your child. This takes a special skill as well as training that not all of these professionals have. Psychologists will often work with an entire family to modify undesirable behaviors in a child with autism.

 Essential

All professionals in the mental health fields have to complete a certain number of hours of professional education annually. Look for a child psychiatrist or psychologist with a special interest in autism. If the professional regularly deals with autism, she should be up-to-date on issues, which should result in better care for your child.

Selecting the Right Physician

The first thing to do is organize your list by geographical convenience; it matters little how good a particular physician may be if you can't get to her office. You don't need to be in your doctor's backyard, but in an emergency, it is nice to have a doctor a few minutes away. It is possible the physician may have more than one office if it is a large practice, in which case knowing what days the doctor is in is helpful. While you are mapping out locations, it is also helpful to make a note of what hours the office is open. Many offices will be open in the evening one night a week to accommodate working parents.

Next, decide if you prefer a male or female physician. It may not matter to you or you may feel more comfortable with a physician of the same sex as your child. If you would be more comfortable with a physician of a certain age, write that in too. Older doctors have more experience but younger doctors may be more open and innovative; it depends on the personality of the physician. If you are uncomfortable asking someone's age, ask how many years she has been in practice.

Then begin interviewing. Call the office to set up an appointment, which should be a free-of-charge visit; tell the receptionist that you would like to schedule a "get acquainted" visit as you are choosing a physician for your child. Note the attitude of the staff on the telephone—in the future, those will be the first people you speak with. They should be friendly, helpful, and professional.

 Alert

Finding the right dentist is extremely important for a child in the autism spectrum. Due to the extreme sensitivity to noise and touch that many of the children have, it is crucial to have a dentist skilled in working with these kids. Many children's hospitals and university medical centers have dental programs for children with special needs.

The physician, when you meet her, should be open and interested in your questions. She should feel no discomfort at being quizzed about how she would handle your child's care and development. You should detect a sense of humor from the prospective doctor but not a flippant attitude. Ask questions specific to your concerns about autism to determine the doctor's level of experience with and interest in ASD. The physician will likely have questions for you, too, and setting up this dialogue is important for the future of your working relationship.

The Importance of Qualified Therapists

Medical care may be only as good as the ancillary medical professionals that provide it. Your child will see different therapists more often than her physician and it is important they are qualified, knowledgeable, and interested in their field. You should be able to tell if the therapists you are seeing care about their work; checking their qualifications is also easy.

Speech Therapists and Audiologists

Audiologists are the head of the team that diagnoses and handles hearing disorders. They may also diagnose and recommend treatment for many communication disorders, but this also can be the role of a speech therapist. When a child has autism, an audiologist is frequently the first professional to see a child, because the parents usually suspect deafness. Audiologists should have at least a master's degree.

 Fact

Audiologists are trained to work with young children and nonverbal children. They will use several techniques to determine if a child has a hearing disorder or a receptive language problem. Although they do not diagnose autism, they are important for ruling out a disorder such as deafness.

Speech therapists, or speech and language pathologists, work with people who have many varied kinds of hearing or communication problems. In an average day, a speech therapist may see a child with a lisp, an older person who has had a stroke, a nonverbal child with autism, and a person with deafness. They work with people of all ages.

Because they work with swallowing disorders as well as speech problems, they can coordinate physical, occupational, and sensory therapies to achieve the maximum results in the time they have with a child. An approach that combines therapies helps bring order to a child's disordered world.

As your child begins therapy, regardless of what method you decide on, you will likely interact with a speech therapist. Talk to the therapist about your concerns regarding language development and what you can do at home to reinforce the therapy. Many small things that you do on a day-to-day basis can incorporate the therapy that is being used to help your child progress.

Physical Therapists

Whether or not your child sees a physical therapist (PT) will depend on her gross motor skills. Many children with autism do not have any deficits in this area and physical therapy is not necessary, but others have extensive issues. The goal of physical therapy is to improve motor functioning. Issues such as range of motion and flexibility are primary concerns that will be addressed by the therapist. PTs work to increase a patient's independence by increasing balance, coordination, and strength.

If your physician recommends a PT, you may find your first visit with him to be much like a doctor visit. PTs will analyze a patient's medical history, conduct an evaluation of their own, and recommend a course of treatment. They will develop an appropriate therapy plan, coordinate all forms of therapy, and instruct parents on home activities to enforce the treatment plan. They may have an assistant work with the patient, but this is not always the case.

PTs are college educated, with a minimum of a master's degree being preferred by most employers. Some states require only a bachelor's degree. They will be certified and belong to a variety of organizations. Continuing education is also a requirement for licensure. As with any kind of therapist, a special interest in autism is helpful.

Occupational Therapists

One of the most important professionals your child will interact with will be the occupational therapist (OT). This person will be pivotal in helping your child build skills or compensate for difficult skills needed for everyday life. The OT may also be referred to as a sensory integration therapist. Like all other therapists your child will work with, this person is college educated and usually has at least two years of training. He will be involved in continuing education, and belong to one or more professional organizations.

 Essential

Many daily living skills are difficult for children with autism to perform. The lack of language, either receptive or expressive, creates difficulty for a child when she isn't sure of what to do or how to do it. An occupational therapist will work with a child to increase fine motor skills but also to increase reasoning and understanding.

An OT will work with a child to teach her to use various tools in her life. All of the skills taught enforce different aspects of mental functioning. A variety of activities will be involved over the course of a child's therapy:

- The use of a computer
- The use of paper and pencil/crayons
- The use of video games to teach hand-eye coordination
- Various exposures to sensory stimuli to decrease overstimulation problems
- Repetitive activities used to teach sequencing
- Flashcards and other language aids used in connection with speech therapy

An OT will do a wide variety of things to increase your child's ability to function independently. If you need something to help your child compensate or adapt, ask the OT. If classroom equipment needs to be modified, the OT will most likely know how to do it. Problem solving is their specialty, and they will bring many solutions to situations that puzzle you.

Licensed Clinical Social Workers

The licensed clinical social worker (LCSW) is no longer exclusively for families who have financial or social problems. The LCSW is a mental-health professional who deals with a variety of emotional and societal issues that bring about conflicts in life. LCSWs are college educated with a master's degree and are required to complete continuing education annually.

If a psychologist can be viewed as treating the mental health of an individual, the LCSW can be considered as the mental-health expert for society. They specialize in maintaining the social functioning of an individual in a group. The LCSW's goal is to create the best social situation possible for your child, whether it is in the family, a group home, or society in general.

Social workers can be helpful when an adult child is considered for placement in a group-home environment. An LCSW will also help a family determine if they are getting the financial help they are entitled to and that it is distributed properly, if that is a concern. They can help a family with many issues at the school level as well. Some LCSWs see people with autism every day and they know the community as well as their clients. As a result, they can assist in making the best decisions for both.

Emerging Treatment Programs

As you explore various options for your child's medical care, you will find many programs and treatment plans. Investigate and research all that are sound and reasonable. But remember, there is presently no cure for autism. Your goal is to make your child the happiest, most well-adjusted person he can be, which is a goal you will hope to be able to reach. Following programs that promise the impossible will not cure autism and will only take your money.

There are many good treatment plans. If you are interested in any form of treatment, consult with your child's physician. It is also helpful to speak with other parents at your support group meeting. Don't try to reinvent the wheel; other people can provide you with a great deal of information. But remember that you must follow your own instincts and do what you think is best for your child and family.

Alert

If something sounds too good to be true, it is. Many people will take advantage of a desperate parent's attempt to find a cure for autism, and people willing to take your money are always available. Even though there are websites and books proclaiming significant improvements with different treatments, not all of these have had their results tested under controlled conditions. So before deciding on alternative therapies, it is wise to discuss them with your autism expert.

Neuro-Immune Dysfunction Syndrome (NIDS) Protocol

Some research has suggested a link between autoimmune disorders, autism, and ADD. NIDS treatment protocol operates to balance the immune system in an effort to reduce the symptoms of autism. The results have been good according to some reports.

The treatment protocol involves looking for various markers including allergens, and viral and bacterial titers. For the patient's family, this means that blood and urine are analyzed for things that the child may be allergic to or that may indicate levels of exposure to certain viruses and bacterial infections. If unusual results are obtained, or allergies are determined, treatment can begin that is said to alleviate some of the symptoms of autism. Treatment begins with allergy medications, antifungals, antivirals, and SSRIs. People on the NIDS protocol are monitored closely with monthly or bimonthly blood work. This treatment would require a child to have considerable blood work and many medications so it should be discussed with an autism expert before a decision is made to try it.

Hyperbaric oxygen treatments are relatively new and some parents have been delighted with the results. However, any treatment such as this should be started only after careful research and discussion with your autism expert.

 Alert

Some therapists use a technique called Greenspan or floortime and also teach this method to parents. The theory is that getting down on the floor with a child will help develop better interaction and communication. Dr. Sidney Greenspan developed this technique and the website to check is *http://stanleygreenspan.com*.

Applied Behavioral Analysis (ABA)

Applied behavioral analysis (ABA), also known as the Lovaas method, is one of the most popular forms of treatment of autism. This therapy does not attempt to reverse a medical condition but has been created instead to change undesirable behaviors into desirable ones. It also teaches social skills, life skills, and encourages language. It builds on small skills, creating bigger skills, and teaching motivation for learning. ABA claims to be effective in modifying the behavior of up to 50 percent of children with autism to the point that they were able to attend a normal classroom without paraprofessional assistance.

ABA is not without controversy. Some fear that children are simply responding to verbal or nonverbal cues and that the behavior mechanizes them. Proponents say that isn't the case if the child is taught properly. There is also a misconception that aversive therapy is used as punishment for undesirable behaviors, when in fact it is not. Unfortunately there is no way to determine which children will be the most responsive and successful with ABA, but younger children who spend more than thirty hours each week in ABA therapy have shown the best results. It requires a great deal of structure within the family but results begin to show quickly, and it is an ideal therapy for many children and their families.

 Essential

Don't ever begin two or more therapies or diets simultaneously. If you have positive results, you will not be certain which treatment or diet was the effective one. Give a new therapy at least three months before you evaluate the results and then decide if you wish to continue.

Diets and Nutrition

Recently there have been many claims about using diet to help decrease some of the symptoms of autism, particularly a child's lack of focus. Some parents and professionals have seen success in two types of nutritional plans: the elimination of gluten and casein, and the addition of B6 vitamins. Following is a discussion of both methods.

The GFCF Diet

One of the most popular treatment plans involves the use of a gluten-free, casein-free (GFCF) diet. This means exactly what it says: A person on this diet ingests no glutens or caseins. It excludes all wheat, rye, barley, and oats from the diet as well as almost all milk products.

To date, the studies conducted on the GFCF diet in autism have been inconclusive, but most have shown promise. Many parents maintain their children on this diet, and the results have been very positive—an amazing 80 percent rate of satisfaction with the treatment plan. It is clear from the research that the need exists for larger and properly designed studies of the possible benefits of this diet in children with autism.

The idea of eliminating gluten and casein from the diet involves a theory that autism could potentially be a metabolic disorder or, as stated earlier, an autoimmune disease. The GFCF diet as a method of treatment is based on the premise that a child with autism is having a toxicological response to the molecule of gluten, and that the central nervous system (CNS) behavior is affected by the action of the molecule in a body that cannot tolerate it. Interestingly, children with celiac disease rarely have autism, but many children with autism have celiac disease.

If you decide to begin this approach to treating autism, do your homework first. Many products have hidden gluten in them, and even one molecule can affect the success of the diet. Learn about gluten-free eating, as it would be a dramatic and difficult change for your family meals. Be aware that a large number of children who do not have autism have a problem with gluten. Your physician can help you determine whether the diet is right for your child and your family.

 Alert

Mealtime can be chaotic and unpleasant if special meals are prepared for each child. Unless a child has a special diet, a bad precedent can be established. Many children both with and without autism will limit their intake to just a few foods. Simple attractive foods should always be offered and junk food or sweets need to be saved for special treats.

Vitamin B$_6$

Vitamin B$_6$ is a very popular form of treatment. It is harmless if taken as directed, and the studies have shown positive results. Individuals require different levels of vitamin B$_6$, and if a person has a deficiency, the theory goes, taking large doses of the vitamin will assist them. If that is the case, autism could also be viewed as a vitamin deficiency, much like scurvy results from a lack of vitamin C. The key is balancing the B_6 intake with the other vitamins to utilize B_6 efficiently without causing a deficiency in another vitamin, which could in turn cause undesirable side effects. Magnesium is used to counteract the larger B_6 intake and has shown to be effective as well. It would be important to discuss any large intake of vitamins with your child's pediatrician.

 Fact

Vitamin B_6 therapy has been thought by some to improve eye contact, reduce self-stimulating behaviors, reduce tantrums, improve social and environmental interactions, and improve speech. If you are interested in this therapy, contact the Autism Research Institute. Your physician may not know about the therapy, so the Institute could send some brochures.

Vitamin B_6 therapy is not a cure—the founders of the treatment will be the first to admit that. But with studies showing at least half of children responding favorably to megadoses of vitamins B_6 and normal supplements of vitamin B complex and magnesium, it is not something parents can easily disregard.

CHAPTER 18

Financial Assistance

Autism can be an expensive condition to deal with. Having good medical coverage is important, but it isn't always easy to come by. Fortunately, there are some ways to get help. Your child may qualify for Social Security benefits. Your understanding of Social Security and how the system works is important in order to have your child evaluated fairly and get the benefits to which you are entitled.

Social Security Benefits

Autism is a "pervasive developmental disorder characterized by social and significant communication deficits originating prior to age twenty-two." It seems hard for many to define autism in just a few words, but the Social Security Administration (SSA) has figured out how to sum it up neatly. They define developmental delay as a "significantly subaverage general intellectual functioning with deficits in adaptive behavior usually manifested before age twenty-two." When a family seeks disability benefits for their child, they will first turn to Social Security. As it is the baseline for the determination of a disability, it is important to understand how the SSA determines if a child is disabled.

Educational and financial decisions may be based on the results of IQ testing on children with autism. This is a very controversial area with parents, as there are concerns about the reliability of an IQ test on a child who has communication deficits.

The Wechsler Adult Intelligence Scale (WAIS) is the primary test that is used by SSA to determine if a person is developmentally delayed. A psychologist or psychiatrist must give the test and interpret the results. The same person must also write an evaluation for SSA stating that the test was valid and accurately reflected the mental status of the individual who was tested. Three areas are tested: verbal, performance, and IQ. The SSA uses the lowest of the three assessments to determine a person's eligibility for benefits. But it is not only the score of the WAIS that factors into this decision, it is also how this score compares to the rest of the population.

 Essential

> IQ testing is an inaccurate measure for determining disability benefits. Instead, a special group of tests should be given by an experienced child psychologist to determine a child's abilities in various areas. Children learn in different ways; some qualify for special education or special help and aids, and tests like these should determine these requirements.

If a child is unable to be evaluated by the WAIS, other tests can be used. The Raven Progressive Matrices is used for people with limited verbal ability and can be helpful for people with autism. The Minnesota Multiphasic Personality Inventory (MMPI) and the Thematic Apperception Test (TAT) are often useful if a child has other brain disorders and can help with supporting those diagnoses.

Supplemental Security Income

If you meet income and asset requirements, your child with autism may qualify for disability support through Social Security.

There was a time that a diagnosis of autism meant an automatic allowance for Supplemental Security Income (SSI), but the recent changes in the laws could mean that parents must prove that their child cannot function "normally" in society in order to be eligible.

Function, Function, Function

Social functioning is a person's ability to relate to and with others. Adults and children have different social skills, but if a person is unable to maneuver through his social environment, he will have difficulty interacting with others in an educational or vocational environment.

Function is a relative term. If you ask a person how your child functions, she may see an entirely different picture from what you see. A physician will see function in one way, and it will be entirely different from how a teacher sees it. This can be frustrating for parents because they see the whole picture and understand exactly what the differences are in people's perceptions of their child. The problem enters in when a disability examiner, who has never met your child, attempts to judge and decide how much of a deficit exists in your child's functioning.

 Alert

Do not allow vague phrases on reports. If a professional states that your child is doing well, meaning that she hasn't had a meltdown in a week, it could be interpreted that there is no longer a severe disability. Ask teachers, doctors, and anyone else who evaluates your child to be as specific as possible.

If you understand what the disability examiner is looking for in order to arrive at a decision, it is easier to offer information that will help him reach the correct conclusion. According to Social Security, a child must have a "marked *and* severe functional limitation," or he is not disabled. The operative word here is "and." It must be both marked and severe, so it is up to the people writing reports and records to show if this is the case. Another phrase that can be an issue is the requirement that a child must have "qualitative deficits in verbal *and* nonverbal communication and in imaginative activity," and again the key word is the same.

Try to view your child as if you were someone who has never seen her before. Does her autism restrict her from participating in activities enjoyed by children of the same age without autism? Does she have communication problems severe enough that she has difficulty expressing what she needs to anyone outside of the family? Does she lack a sense of danger? Is she unable to care for herself in a socially appropriate manner? If you answer yes to these questions, it is your job as your child's advocate to see that this information is conveyed to Social Security effectively and accurately.

Presenting an Accurate Picture

Knowing how the severity of your child's disability will be determined is the most important piece of information you have. Medical sources, as well as educational and social sources, can be used to support your claim that your child is disabled. This includes reports on how she lives her daily life: how she functions with others, her attention span, obsessive behaviors, tantrums, aggression, and other issues in her life that interfere with typical functioning. You can submit reports from any source you deem appropriate. These statements can be from immediate or extended family members, day care staff, community service workers, respite care workers, or any other person involved with your child on a regular basis.

Keep in mind that children, particularly children with autism, change from day to day and month to month. Your child's behavior tomorrow may be different from what it was today. In a report, you want to convey an overall impression. Do not let the temptation of making your child look good take over as you collect these reports. Save that for Sunday school. What you want now is to accurately prove the deficits in her ability to function. If she functions in a manner that prohibits her from having a life similar to other children, she is eligible, and you need to prove it. What must be conveyed is how she functions *now*, not how you hope she will function in the future.

How to Apply for SSI

Applying for benefits is not difficult but it is a tedious and time-consuming process. The best way to proceed is to organize your financial records and all of the medical documentation you have so that it is at hand when you begin the application. The application process will include the following steps:

1. Gather all your documentation in advance: a certified copy of your child's birth certificate, tax and earnings records, name and address of medical and educational providers, and contact information for anyone who sees your child regularly.

2. Call Social Security at 800-772-1213, or go to a local office if there is one in your area, and request forms for the application of Childhood Disability Benefits.

3. Fill out all forms completely and accurately. It sometimes helps to photocopy the forms first so you can use one as a "practice sheet."

4. Notify all people you have listed on the forms that they will be receiving requests for written reports, and notify physician and school offices that records will be requested. Reiterate the importance of providing accurate information.

5. About three weeks after submitting the forms to Social Security, contact them to follow up on what records and reports they have received and which ones are missing.

6. Follow up on missing reports and provide any additional information the disability examiner may need.

Unfortunately, the SSI process can be a tedious one. Many parents feel like the disability examiners are there to disallow any application, but don't let this get in your way. The odds are high you will be rejected on the first try unless your child is profoundly autistic or has other medical conditions; this shouldn't stop you from attempting to get her disability allowed. If you are rejected, you can appeal and it is quite common for disallowed cases to be allowed after review. If you are approved on appeal, your child's benefits will be backdated to the date that the claim was disallowed, which can be a sizeable sum of money that will help offset the expenses you have incurred since then.

 Fact

Problems not easily solved may require the services of a disability advocate or attorney. Special-education attorneys are available through some nonprofit agencies. The Protection and Advocacy organization has offices throughout the United States. Their website is *www.protectionandadvocacy.com.*

Medical Coverage

There are few things more important than medical coverage, particularly when a family member has a disorder such as autism. Unfortunately, most private insurances have had an exclusion for autism and would not cover anything that is in any way related to the diagnosis of an autism spectrum disorder. With the new health care bill this should change. However, it is important to check on the following:

- When you call a doctor for an appointment for your child, tell the receptionist why you want the physician to see your child. If it is a sore throat, for example, tell them that at the time you make the appointment.

- If your physician's office has a sign-in form, sign your child's name and write down the reason for your child's visit, even if there is not a place on the form for that information.
- When the nurse or other staff member comes into the examination room and asks the reason for the visit, if it is not related to autism, there is no reason to state that your child has autism. Unless it is a physician you have not seen before, your doctor knows your child has autism.
- When the doctor sees your child, be certain to stress at the beginning of the visit that autism is not your reason for being there.
- Upon leaving the office, you may be presented with a copy of the insurance slip. Check the section for diagnosis and be sure autism is not circled or written in—it is an irrelevant diagnosis if the problem was a sore throat or another unrelated condition.

Many physicians and their staff include all the diagnoses a person has on an insurance form, without realizing that only the diagnosis pertinent to the visit should be documented. Strep throat or a checkup has nothing to do with autism, and your insurance should cover it just as it would with any other family member.

 Essential

The disabled adult-children's benefits, through Social Security, are available to adult children who were disabled prior to age twenty-two. Their parents must no longer be able to provide for them due to retirement, disability, or death. These benefits can help offset expenses later in life.

One of the reasons SSI is so important is because with SSI comes Medicaid if you are in the income bracket that qualifies for

Medicaid. This is a state-funded health insurance that does not exclude autism-related visits from its coverage. Even if your SSI drops to a level that seems hardly worth having, you should still have Medicaid to ease your financial burden. If you have no other medical coverage for autism, keeping Medicaid should be high on your list of priorities. You will still have to qualify for Medicaid by meeting certain income requirements, but it would be a consideration in your financial planning.

Creative Financial Assistance

Parents need to take a proactive approach and find ways to secure financial assistance as they deal with the cost of autism. For example, parents may not be able to afford home health care, but if their income is below a certain level, they can have home health aides paid for by Medicare or Medicaid. They will need a prescription from a physician.

Different States, Different Help

Throughout the United States, different assistance programs and benefits are available. Each of these depends on the state in which you live. Although most assistance comes from a federally funded program, it is administrated on state levels, and each of the fifty states has its own regulations.

Some states have programs known as Family Support Funds. The Developmental Disability Center (DDC) in each state manages these funds. Qualifying is easy, and parents are usually taken on their word about a child's disability. Payments can be as low as $500 a year and as high as $500 a month. The only requirement is that the funds distributed to each family must be used for the benefit of the child with the disability. Call the local DDC and ask about funds of this nature. If you are unable to find any resources, ask members of your support group, who will likely know what is available.

Additionally, when you file your state income tax, find out if there is another deduction for your child's disability. Some states allow two deductions for a child with autism or another disability. Check into your state's laws to be sure you are receiving every tax benefit possible.

 Fact

If you are on the lower end of the income scale, you still have a potential tax benefit. The Earned Income Credit (EIC) may give you a refund larger than the taxes you pay! This program was put in place to assist what the government terms the "working poor" and can help single-parent families as well as families struggling to get by each month.

A True Tax Incentive

There are ways to save money on your taxes. Deductions are available to most families, and although filing with itemized deductions is more complex, it can make a big difference. Itemizing deductions means using the actual expenses you have incurred throughout the previous year instead of the government-estimated standard deduction. You will need to keep all of the receipts as proof of your expenditures. You can deduct anything that is necessary to treat the medical condition of any member of your family, such as:

- Health insurance costs paid by you for medical, dental, and prescription coverage
- Physician visits that you pay for and are not covered by insurance
- Co-payments required for medical services
- Medical equipment necessary and prescribed and not covered by insurance for any member of your family

- Deductibles on your health insurance for which you are financially responsible
- Contact lenses and glasses as well as the supplies that are needed to care for them
- Prescribed birth control
- Insulin and other medicines
- Transportation to medical care or therapy

Remember, if you can reduce the amount you owe in federal taxes, you will also be reducing your state income tax. It would be wise to speak with a tax expert or accountant with a good understanding of laws regarding disabilities. This person will be able to help you get maximum benefits and find the best options for your family.

 Fact

It is the nature of people to not want to accept financial assistance. But you have paid taxes for many years, and these taxes were intended for social programs to help people in need. Do not feel guilty about accepting benefits that you are due.

Respite Care

By the time some parents hear about respite care, they are already exhausted and burned out. No one can do it all, but parents of children with autism seem compelled to attempt it, and they generally do quite well. The autism community has many remarkable parents who have been tested by fire and come out stronger for it. But everyone needs a break from autism, and that includes you.

A Service for the Whole Family

Respite care gives both caregiver and the person with a disability a break from the daily routine of being together. It is beneficial for the child, and it is essential for the parent. A special-needs child is not an independent element in your household. Everyone in the family is affected by his needs, and you will spend a lifetime accomplishing this adjustment. This is why respite care is a family service; it is there to assist the entire family as they care for a disabled child at home.

If your child is newly diagnosed, you may not be able to even consider leaving him with another individual. This is a normal reaction and you shouldn't do anything that makes you feel uncomfortable. There will be a time you will be open to the idea, but in the meantime, just keep it in the back of your mind as an option. Don't dismiss the idea completely for now, and be sure to sign up if there is a waiting list in your area through the various agencies. You can always turn it down later if you don't feel you need it or aren't ready to try leaving your child.

 Essential

Respite care is beneficial for your child as well as for you. Having other people take charge at times will put some variety in your child's life and teach her that she can, and should, communicate with others. Work with the respite caregiver so she understands the communication system your child uses.

Finding a Respite Caregiver

When you consider respite-care options, have a list of questions ready. Will the care be provided in your home or in another place? What kind of costs are involved and what type of assistance is available? You will want to know how a service selects respite caregivers and what kind of training they have and if they are experienced in first aid and CPR. Health and Human Services or the social workers you work with can guide you in finding the respite care that is appropriate for your family. Ask if you can meet the respite caregiver who will be assigned to your child before your child meets her. It is also important, because of the routine people with autism have, to know if the same caregiver will be available each time for your child. It could be once a month or twice a month that you get to take advantage of respite care. It can also be weekly. You will be provided services based on your family's needs and the availability of respite caregivers in your area.

As your child matures into adulthood, respite care can be used to assist in the building of skills. Considering that most minimally functioning adults with autism live in a group-home environment, the experience of respite care can help families with the transition if that time arrives. There are many services and resources available; it is just a matter of discovering them. You will likely be able to find something with which you are comfortable.

Custody Issues

It seems almost inconceivable, but in the recent past, because of the lack of affordable medical care and insurance, 20 percent of families were forced to make a decision about parental rights. The choice? Whether to retain custody of their child or give up custody to the state in order to acquire medical care for the child. The reason? The family either lacked medical insurance, or there were exclusions on their medical insurance policy relating to the child's condition requiring care.

In 2002, it was estimated by the General Accounting Office of the federal government that 13,000 children were given up by their families to be placed into child welfare or various other parts of the "system." Some were put into the care of juvenile justice, even though they had committed no crime. Their parents just couldn't afford their medical care or there were no services available in their community. This did not affect only families with children who had autism, but families with any disabled children as well.

Much of the problem was part of the overall health care crisis in the United States that necessitated the need for change. It is hoped that the provisions in the new health care bill will prevent these things from happening in the future.

The economic problems today reach into the school system with special education funds being cut, despite the fact that the numbers of children with autism continues to increase. But the true tragedy, the true fallout for society occurs when families cannot care for their children with autism.

If you have a child that has been recently diagnosed with autism, begin financial planning now so that a custody issue is never a problem you will have to face. Savings, whole-life insurance policies, and equity in a home are just some of the options that can protect you financially.

CHAPTER 19

Support for Parents

It is not uncommon for parents to feel a sense of isolation when they learn their child has autism. Autism is a word that seems very final and is as one parent said, "The most devastating of disabilities." After some time passes you will feel less that way, and you will learn it is not the most devastating thing that can happen. Isolation is not something you have to learn to live with and, in fact, you shouldn't. There are many forms of support available to you that are worth taking advantage of.

The Importance of Support

Are you the tough go-it-alone type? Do you resist sharing openly about your fears and the concerns you have? Are you the kind of person who can't imagine discussing your personal life in a group setting? If so, you will likely find that the journey through autism is a bit bewildering and lonely. Remember that looking for support does not make a person weak. Rather, it creates a foundation of stability and knowledge that imparts security and confidence.

When the Muppets were at the height of their popularity, the show featured a segment that was intended to entertain and impress people with the creativity of the puppet. It involved a centipede, and not an ordinary centipede but a very special Muppet centipede with fabulous clothes and fifty pairs of oversized shoes. He had a colorful jacket, a small suitcase, a hat with a flower on it, and a very big umbrella. He sang a complete rendition of "You'll Never Walk Alone" and although the skit was humorous, there was a great deal of truth and meaning in it. How can you ever get all those feet, all 100 of them, organized and coordinated enough to walk together?

The answer is simple: You can't. But you don't have to walk this journey alone. The centipede, looking at a higher power for authority, had the right idea. He knew he couldn't possibly coordinate all his feet, make his way through a thundering rainstorm without losing his suitcase, and still make his destination safely if he didn't have some help. He needed support. So, he sang his song and kept plugging away. And he made it in one piece; because of the support he had, he was able to travel his treacherous journey.

Autism is much like that. You may feel like the centipede at times as you try to coordinate your feet upon a path you didn't know you would have to walk. You may be drenched with the rain as everything around you is falling down, and you may think your little umbrella is going to blow inside out as it tries to shelter you. But out there, beyond your immediate surroundings, there is a full orchestra playing with an entire chorus of people singing the same song. They already know the words and the way to walk to this music.

What Is Support?

Seeking support is letting others teach you how to walk and sing that same song the others are already singing. It is also teaching others what you have learned when you are confident in your abilities. Support is making it happen with the help of others who have "been there, done that." Support is learning to ask questions that you didn't even know existed. And support is the only way you are going to get through this.

A lot of the reason parents have problems with getting their own parents to understand what a struggle autism can be at times is simply a lack of knowledge heightened by a failure to communicate. You may approach your own mother with your frustrations, but she has no frame of reference, having not had nor raised a child with autism herself. Your frustration will be received as a question, whether you intend it that way or not, and like most moms, she will attempt to help. This just makes the situation worse, because her suggestions probably won't work; it's not her fault. She doesn't know because how could she?

Getting Support

This is the advantage of a support group. Those people know! They have been right where you are and you don't have to explain the entire autism spectrum to them in order to vent a little. Few things are more frustrating than needing to have a gripe session, but before you can launch into your frustration, having to give a twenty-minute speech to explain the issues that have caused your frustration to begin with.

 Fact

If you need to find a physician or dentist, ask at your support group meeting. The people there will have suggestions and will be able to give you their opinion of the care their child received. Recommendations from people who may share concerns similar to yours are a great way to find the services your child needs.

A support group for families who have children with autism won't mind if you stagger into a meeting exhausted from a lack of sleep because your child only slept for thirty minutes the night before. They may have been up all night, too. They understand you need to find a babysitter who can handle autism for two hours so you can attend one of your other children's school conferences. They probably even have a list of names and phone numbers.

Above all, a support group, just by its presence, will remind you that you aren't alone in your daily struggles. You will learn that they, too, worry about what will happen when their child is an adult—they have the same fears and concerns you have. They will reassure you that you did nothing to cause this to happen to your child and will rejoice with your victories and cry with your disappointments. They truly will move in the same orbit and will depend on you just as you depend on them.

Giving Support

As time goes by and autism and all its idiosyncrasies become second nature to you, you will find that you have a lot of knowledge and experience to impart to others. For some people it happens immediately and for others it takes a bit longer. You will go from being an observer, to a listener, to being a parent that helps parents with newly diagnosed children. You will have ideas, solutions, and little tricks you have stumbled upon that will be of invaluable help to someone you may not even know yet

 Alert

One rule that should be followed in any support group is not to criticize other people for their decisions about treatment and therapy for autism. Keep your comments and opinions positive and helpful. Every person is entitled to his or her opinion and should be treated with respect.

The most important thing you can remember about giving support is to withhold judgment. It is possible that you will meet someone who has different theories from yours on the causes and the best treatments for autism. These are unknowns right now, and it is more important to work together on coping than to spend valuable time and energy debating the issues. No one is totally right and no one is totally wrong. Autism support groups are full of parents trying to get by and do the best job they possibly can, and what they need is encouragement.

Much of dealing with autism is learning by trial and error. Participating in a support group allows you to learn from the experience of others; you will save a lot of frustration and irritation if you can avoid the mistakes others have made. When you have had some experience, then you can share what you have learned and help others as they begin their journey.

Finding the Right Support Group

Just as every treatment isn't right for your child, not every support group will be right for you. Some support groups are founded on a belief in a certain treatment. If you do not feel comfortable with the particular treatment that is the foundation for a support group, it won't be a good fit for you. They provide specialized support for those who follow a certain theory, and that is fine, but don't ever join a group with the idea that you can change its focus. That isn't fair to them or you.

What Are the Differences?

There are many different kinds of support groups available. There are large ones and small ones, ones that meet weekly and ones that meet monthly, ones with and without babysitting provided, and ones that serve particular age groups. There is no one right way to have a support group. The goal is to create a community or family where the issues of raising a child with autism can be freely discussed.

If you have never been part of a support group, consider joining one that is general in its nature and approach. Their main emphasis should be on coping with autism and its behaviors, not to advocate a specific theory.

General Disabilities or ASD Specific?

One of the first decisions to make in selecting the right support group for you is whether you want a group for parents of children with any disability or one that is only for parents of children with autism. There are good things about either type of group. Some of this may depend on the community in which you live—it may be hard to find a very specific support group if you live in a small town.

Groups that support families who have children with various disabilities bring a great deal of variety into a discussion and add to the group dynamics. If you have never been to a support meeting, you may think you would have little in common with a mother holding a baby that depends on a feeding tube. You will be surprised at how much you do have in common once you begin to talk and learn about each other's daily lives. Parents of deaf children will have a lot of advice about handling simple communication issues; even though their children may have receptive speech, they know what a lack of expressive speech means to a family.

 Essential

> Walking into a support meeting for the very first time can be a little scary, but remember that everyone there is looking forward to meeting you and your family. Get there early so others walk in when you are already there and it will seem easier.

One of the most significant benefits of a group that supports various disabilities is the way it will dispel your sense of isolation. When you see other parents dealing with issues far different from yours, yet just as disabling, and realize these parents are surviving, you will no longer feel as alone. Meeting people who deal with children who are physically and mentally challenged puts life into perspective and things become more manageable for all involved.

Groups that support only parents of children with autism also offer some great benefits. Parents who deal with autism on a daily basis are not going to so much as lift an eyebrow if your child empties out your purse and lines up its contents on the floor. That is "standard operating procedure" to those parents. They know what a meltdown is and won't stare at you when your child demonstrates one right in the middle of the parking lot as you are leaving. They understand elopement and how fearful it is. And they won't assume your child will talk to them; they will understand the limitations of a nonverbal child.

Specialized Groups

After some time, if you become involved in a particular treatment, you can even seek out a group that is devoted to discussion of that treatment. They will likely touch on general coping strategies as well, but their thrust will center on a particular therapy. One advantage to a specialized support group is the information you can obtain from the experiences of the members. If you, for example, want to try a particular diet to treat your child's autism, it can be helpful to be around people who are using that eating plan. There is no reason to reinvent the wheel, so be there to learn and eventually share with others.

All types of support groups have strong points that should be considered. It is likely that a group for general disabilities will have some families who have children with autism in the group. You may be limited in your choices because of location or scheduling issues, but keep looking until you find one that works for you. Making it a point to join and regularly attend a support group is one step you can take that will help your life immensely.

Forming a Support Group

If you have discovered that there is no support group in your local area, you might consider starting one of your own. You have the qualifications as the parent of a child on the autism spectrum. Beginning a support group is easy and takes a minimum of time and money.

Begin by talking with your child's physician. She might want to get involved on some level and at the very least will tell other patients about the group. Also, speak with the special-education department at the school your child attends or will be attending. You do not need their approval, but it would be helpful to have them involved. If you live near a community mental health center, connecting with them would be helpful, too.

Organizing

After you have some experts aware of your support group's "birth," begin to organize by setting preliminary schedules and goals. Meeting once a week is standard practice; you can also have special functions when the group is established, but for now start with weekly meetings. Compare your schedule to other schedules in your community to look for potential conflicts; if every religious center in town has a Wednesday night service, choose another evening.

 Fact

Churches or other religious centers could be a good place for support group meetings. If you are a member of a church, synagogue, or mosque, ask if they would be willing to donate a room for a meeting. Have members bring soft drinks, water, cookies, and muffins and you will be all ready to go.

Your next step is to find a space that would work for your meeting. Your local library may have a room they will let you use at no charge. Senior centers and community meeting halls are also possibilities. Your home is an option but it should be your last choice;

you don't want the stress of making your home "just-so" when you want to create a supportive environment for families. Make fliers and posters to let people know where and when you will be meeting.

The next step is easy. Put out cookies, coffee, and tea, and wait for people. They will show up if you have the word out. Spend time getting to know people and let your group evolve naturally. You can have guest speakers if you want and think it would be helpful. Many large support groups have started from small beginnings such as this. You may be creating a new family!

Activities for Support Groups

Many groups have planned activities. They may be educational or just for fun. They can be to raise money to help the support group in different ways or to funnel toward an autism awareness fund that the group would like to support. Whatever your goals, plan ahead to get as much out of the activity as possible.

Guest speakers should be scheduled about three months or more before you would like them to speak. That will allow you to organize discussions that work up to the speaker's topic and create greater interest. When you contact someone about speaking to your group, ask about fees and what topic they would like to discuss. If fees are involved you may be able to cover them with a fund you have for this purpose. If there is a speaker you really want to bring in but the fee is higher than your budget, plan a fundraiser to cover the expenses.

Annual activities, such as a holiday party or a summer picnic, are common in groups that meet regularly. A yearly calendar can help your group stay organized, especially when an annual event requires a lot of advance planning. Picnics often require that an area of a park be reserved, and holiday parties will need a comfortable space for adults and children of all ages. Again, you may want to establish a fund to cover such activities.

Another activity that your group might take advantage of is attending a national autism seminar. Throughout the year, many such seminars are held for two to four days. If two or three of your group attend and bring back notes and information they could share with the rest of the group, it could be helpful for everyone. Groups will sometimes plan for one seminar yearly and coordinate a fundraising event to cover the expenses.

 Alert

A great way to generate funds for your support group is to have all the families get together for a combined garage sale. If everyone donates to the sale and helps with advertising and set-up, your group could make a substantial amount of money that could be used for various activities.

All support groups are different, so the activities of each one will vary, but one thing is true across the board. Lifetime friendships are created in these groups. The more you can contribute to your support group, the more you will receive in return. Special activities serve to educate and bind people together as they work toward common goals.

Support on the Internet

The Internet may be one of the greatest inventions of the twentieth century. Never before in human history can so many people be instantly in contact in any part of the world at any time of the day or night. The cost of the equipment is reasonable and the wealth of information you can find online is staggering. If you need it, or want it, or have to understand it, you can find it online. If you don't have a computer, your public library will have several you can use for short periods of time.

A Microcosm

Many people who have not yet ventured onto the Internet are hesitant and sometimes a bit fearful. They worry they won't understand it and are concerned about the dangers the media presents. Others do not think any valid information can be found on websites and therefore have not investigated the available resources. Others are "technophobes" and do not do well with what they perceive to be advanced technology.

Rest assured the Internet is no more than a microcosm of the "real world." It is no different from the rest of your world; it just reflects society. As in the real world, the Internet has good neighborhoods and bad neighborhoods. It has people you can trust and care for and it has people to be avoided. It has good Samaritans and it has thieves. As one child with autism proudly exclaimed as he began to grasp the concept of the computer and Internet, "There's a bunch of people in there!!"

Online Autism Communities

An autism community on the Internet is much like any other community. It has information, people, discussions, planned meetings, chat rooms, shopping, and many personal opinions from the community population, as well as medical professionals. You can find resources that can be trusted; just remember to pay attention to the source of the information.

One of the major advantages to autism communities on the Internet is the accessibility factor. They are literally open twenty-four hours a day, seven days a week. They are good for middle-of-the-night ranting and raving, and they are wonderful for people who live in isolated areas. If you have a work schedule that prohibits your attending a real-life support group, the Internet is your next best bet. And if you have a real-life support group, the knowledge you gain on the Internet can enhance your group meetings.

Appendix B at the end of this book has sources on the Internet that are valuable for anyone close to a child with autism. If you are new to the world of cyberspace, find a good book to help you get around on the web and find the resources you are searching for. Check out various communities and discover the volume of information that can help you as you learn about autism.

Other Online Communities

There are many communities on the Internet that you will find useful. Don't limit yourself to sites just related to autism. There are many other resources to help you take care of yourself and meet your own needs, and your children will benefit from it.

Communities for spirituality can be helpful for people who feel that the spiritual part of their lives must be functional for their lives to be complete. There are many sites for every faith known that are managed by people who believe as you do. Joining such a community will enrich your own life and, by extension, the lives of your children.

If you are a news junkie, the Internet is the place to be. All of the major news services can be found online as well as thousands of reliable news sources that may be brand new to you. Sometimes parents become so involved with a child's disability, they forget to stay in touch with the rest of the world. On the Internet, you can do that at your convenience, not on a television network's schedule.

If you have a need or are just looking for something for fun, if it is for business or entertainment, or if you are looking for something for yourself or for your children, you will be able to find a community for it online. Use search engines to find what you are looking for and just see where it might take you.

Mailing Lists and Newsletters

One primary method for communication used online by support groups is known as a mailing list. This is like a discussion that is spread out over a period of time. People subscribe to a mailing list and e-mails are generated from one person to the entire group. Any number of people can answer a given e-mail, and their response goes out to all members of the list. It is much like standing in the middle of a party and carrying on several conversations at once. People on mailing lists tend to become friends and sometimes even expand their friendships off the list, sometimes meeting in real life.

Newsletters are another source of information for parents of children who are disabled. Websites will often have a weekly, biweekly, or monthly newsletter that is e-mailed to subscribers at no charge. The benefit of these newsletters is that someone else is doing the research for you. All you have to do is visit the site where they have the information posted. This can be a great service but be sure that any newsletters you receive are sent by sources you can trust.

Easier Living on the Net

The Internet can make life much easier for a family that has a child with a disability. There are features that can help you take care of responsibilities without having to ever leave the house. Many banks are online and allow full banking to be done on their website. Credit cards can be paid online, as can most utilities. There are services through many banks that will pay all the bills you request and you don't need stamps, envelopes, or a parking place.

There are also many sources for shopping. This is especially convenient if you live in a small area that doesn't have all of the retail outlets you might need. Books, music, gifts, clothes, pets, supplies for anything, and jewelry are just some of the examples of what you can find. This can be convenient for holiday shopping; taking a child with autism to a mall is difficult and stressful. Now you can bring the mall to you.

Being Cautious

Using the same common sense you use in your everyday life will prevent problems online. You wouldn't walk down a busy city street with a purse or wallet hanging open, so don't give your credit card information to a site that is not legitimate. Remember, there are people who are not reputable waiting to sell you the latest "cure" for autism, just as there are people on city streets selling things that are questionable. Just because it is legal doesn't mean it is a wise purchase. Just be practical and learn as much as you can about the environments you visit online, and it will be a positive and helpful experience.

CHAPTER 20

The Future of Autism

The autism community is very diverse. There is no race, no religion, and no economic class unaffected by autism spectrum disorders. Male or female? Autism doesn't care—it is an equal opportunity disorder. This diverse community is struggling to make the best lives they can for their children who have autism. What will this mean for the futures of those with autism?

Struggling for Unity

While parents struggle daily with autism, another problem, in some ways more insidious, enters their life. The struggle for a united front in the autism community is an issue that has yet to be conquered. The lack of unity has divided people to the point that their "strength in numbers" has substantially been diluted. And because there is no unity in approaching research, each of the major autism organizations supports research efforts just in their own area of concern.

With this disjointed approach, the pharmaceutical industry views autism as a condition that does not need extensive research efforts, especially since those who have the greatest stake in finding a cure cannot agree. Federal health agencies, for example, share responsibility for dealing with autism, but each agency deals with a separate part of the picture and protects its own little piece of the research pie. This does not appear to be the case in many other childhood illnesses. There are also many illnesses that affect fewer children than autism does and yet get more attention from researchers working to develop treatments and cures.

In order to advance the quest toward finding a cure or at least a treatment for autism, the autism organizations, federal government, and medical community must put aside their own special interests and take a unified approach to the issues involved. But, before that will happen, parents need to look at themselves and their support system. The lack of unity begins at the level of the family and with dissension and conflict, moves out from there.

The Role of the Individual

People do not intend to divide the autism community; it is a situation that began many years ago and is now self-sustaining. The divisions, and all the hostile feelings around it, have infected support groups, online forums, newsletters, and almost anywhere the autism community meets for information and support. Support groups are there to help ease a burden and when people begin verbally assaulting each other, it delays progress in autism issues that much more. If someone insists that they are right about their beliefs about the cause of autism, and that you are wrong, just ignore it.

 Alert

Online verbal assaults are called "flaming." If you are verbally attacked for what you think, don't acknowledge it. The Internet gives people a feeling of anonymity and things are said that might not be said in person. No one will change his opinion and arguing just ratchets up the stress level.

Parents do not have to agree on the cause of autism. They do not have to argue and debate endlessly on vaccinations, diet, genetics, or what star was in which quadrant that day. At the end of the day, it doesn't matter who is right. What matters is that the autism community unites so that research can find the answers. It is important that we find the best treatment for each child, because very soon these children will be adults, and society will not be prepared.

If parents can unify on a grass-roots level, this will eventually influence the actions of people who can make the decisions to provide the funds for more research. Bickering will never gain one iota of information and only harms the people that are being bickered about: the children.

Looking for Answers

Of course, finding an answer necessitates finding a cause that can be agreed upon. Researchers in different parts of the world are forming theories on the cause of autism and potential treatments. Scientific studies continue with some of the world's most dedicated researchers determined to unlock the autism puzzle. Someday the cause, the prevention, and the treatment will be discovered. It could be sometime this year or it may not happen for decades; as nebulous as the questions and answers are, the question of how long this may take is even less clear.

In the meantime, coping is the best any parent or caregiver can do. No magic bullet has come along yet and life must go on. Look for answers but don't become so wrapped up in finding the answer that you forget the question. Until a 100 percent preventative treatment is found, the important question is, and always will be, "How can I raise this child to be the happiest person with autism that she can be?"

Too Much Autism
The parents of children with autism are some of the most patient and giving people on the planet. They have had to deal

with a lot; the loss they have experienced is ever-present, yet they respond with good nature, skill, and love. But there is a trap you might fall into, and preventing it can be a lot easier than escaping from it. It can affect any parent of a child with any disability, but is more prevalent in parents of children with autism. And it is common for parents not to recognize that they are in the trap. The trap could be called "Too Much Autism."

When parents suffer from too much autism, their lives can spin out of control. The traits of parents with too much autism include:

- Surfing the Internet for hours each day looking for treatments.
- Depression beginning with the diagnosis and lasting for six months or more.
- Arguing with people who have differing views on cause and treatment for autism. Debate is one thing, but public disputes that get out of hand are not helpful to anyone.
- Unwillingness to enjoy their own activities and hobbies because it takes them away from their child.
- Having a need to discuss autism for several hours each day, which can be difficult for friends and family.

Your Attitude Counts

If you find yourself thinking, "How do I possibly have a normal life after this? How can I do anything less?" you need to readjust your thinking. There is no such thing as a "normal" life—everyone has his or her own life with its good luck, bad luck, and just plain strange luck. Don't let autism take over your life. It is a big part of your life and, certainly, of your child's life. But you are not defined by autism and neither is your child.

And as hard as it is, as cold as it sounds, you need to remember that while your child does have this condition, you do not. Many parents, particularly mothers, subconsciously feel the need to punish themselves for their child's condition. If a mom limits her own life to "autism and her child," then she will share in the burden of autism, receiving what she feels is her just penance.

 Essential

> It is normal to search for information on a diagnosis your child receives; but when you constantly search you risk encountering bad information, unscrupulous people, and promised cures with no validity whatsoever—and you may lose your sense of objectivity to evaluate the information. The worst effect, though, will be the loss of hope.

If only it were that easy; if only parents could punish themselves and remove the struggle from their children. Any parent would cheerfully submit to that penalty if it worked. But not participating in things you love to do, ignoring your normal social life, and giving up your career is not going to make your child better. Letting your marriage slide and not tending it carefully is not going to make autism go away. Autism is like grief—you can't make it go away and you never get over it, but you can learn to live with it or adjust to the situation.

The Impact on Society

It is shocking enough to realize that autism once occurred with a frequency of 1 per 15,000, but now it shows an increase to 1 per 100 or 1 per 150. The sheer increase in numbers of children diagnosed with autism since 1990 is alarming.

Is society ready to provide services for that many people with autism? Can the United States handle the financial load? If autism continues to remain poorly understood, can society take the social impact that will without a doubt occur as a result of so many people with communication and social deficits? Sociologists will be working hard with psychologists and physicians to determine the answers to these questions. None of this will be figured out quickly, and much of it will be learned by trial and error. Unfortunately, it will be at the expense of children with autism and their families.

 Fact

> The numbers of cases of autism and autism spectrum disorders, appear to be growing. Society cannot escape the impact of this rise in numbers, which can almost be considered an epidemic. Now over 500,000 kids and teens under age twenty-one fit into the autism spectrum.

Societies, and even civilizations, are measured by how they treat children, the disabled, and the elderly. If this old proverb is true, then the United States has a less than satisfactory report card. Yet there are no easy answers. In a perfect world, we would find the cause, and then treatment and prevention. But a perfect world may be a long way off.

In the meantime, parents need to take the knowledge they have gained through their experiences and educate others who are not exposed to autism. The impact on our society cannot be overstated, and only parents, by bringing autism to the public table, can ease the burden. You are your child's best advocate, but now you are also an ambassador for autism.

Awareness Issues

You may have noticed that there is no national telethon for autism. People do not gather around the television with open wallets for disorders on the autism spectrum. Many people have never heard of it, and those who have often know only the misconceptions provided by films and television.

Funding for research is sadly limited. If any other disease or situation affected such a large number of children, it would be considered a national emergency. For some reason the attention isn't there for autism.

Why isn't it? "We need an 'in your face' approach," one father said. "Don't people realize that they aren't affected by autism because they dodged the bullet? It could be any child in any family at any time." An "in your face" approach may be what it takes to increase awareness, funding, and services for these children.

 Essential

Autism is being discussed as never before. Because of the tireless efforts of many organizations and individuals, people are becoming more aware, not only of the disorder but also of the people who live with it each and every day of their lives. But we must keep up efforts to spread the information to even more people.

Parents need to start asking questions and expecting answers. Until we know what has caused this condition and how to treat it, coping and making a child with autism the "happiest, most well-adjusted child with autism he can be" is critical.

Some researchers and "experts" in the field have stated that autism has not increased but the methods of diagnosis have improved, thus causing the statistics to rise. However, to most parents and educators, this theory makes no sense. If society simply overlooked or misdiagnosed autistic children of previous generations, there should be more adults recognized as having autism, but this hasn't been the case.

Every April is Autism Awareness Month. Every year autism societies, support groups, parents, and journalists make extraordinary efforts to draw public attention to the problem of autism. Autism ribbons are showing up and every time someone asks what the colorful puzzle ribbon is, another person learns about autism. Keep learning, and keep sharing what you know with others, and you'll do your part to increase public awareness of the urgency of this problem.

Glossary

Activities of daily living (ADL)
The activities that each person engages in daily for personal care and hygiene. Dressing and bathing are examples.

American Sign Language (ASL)
The primary sign language used in the United States. It was developed for people with deafness and is often conceptually based.

Applied behavioral analysis (ABA)
A therapy method that uses positive reinforcement to encourage appropriate behaviors that will help an individual with autism function in society. Also called the Lovaas method, after Dr. Ivar Lovaas.

Asperger's Syndrome (AS)
A disorder on the autism spectrum characterized by normal speech and social difficulties. Diagnosis may not occur until the child is older.

Aspie
A person with Asperger's Syndrome.

Attention deficit disorder (ADD)
A developmental disorder that is characterized by a short attention span and a lack of concentration on tasks.

Attention deficit hyperactivity disorder (ADHD)
A developmental disorder that is composed of ADD and hyperactivity in the same individual.

Auditory processing disorder (APD)
A disorder in which language is heard correctly but not understood or not processed correctly by the brain.

Augmentative and alternative communication (AAC)
A communication aid to assist people with limited or no verbal ability. A communication board is the most commonly used tool.

Autism
A neurological disorder characterized by communication difficulties, sensory problems, and socialization issues. Usually appears between eighteen and twenty-four months.

Autism Society of America (ASA)
One of the leading autism organizations in the United States.

Autism spectrum disorders (ASD)
A collection of disorders characterized by symptoms such as impaired verbal ability and social dysfunction.

Beneficiary
The recipient of a trust fund, life insurance policy, or other assets and funds that have been designated to go to that person.

Diagnostic and Statistical Manual of Mental Disorders, (DSM-IV)

A publication used to diagnose autism spectrum and other disorders. The fourth edition is the most current version.

Echolalia

The verbal repetition of words without using those words for any communication or meaning.

Elopement

The tendency of a child with autism to "escape" her environment and wander off, usually with no particular direction in mind.

Encopresis

A bowel disorder where very hard stool forms in the rectum and liquid stool leaks out around it.

Exact Sign Language

A form of sign language using much of American Sign Language that has a sign for each word. Also known as "Exact English."

Expressive speech

The ability to utilize spoken language to convey ideas, thoughts, and feelings.

Facilitated communication

A controversial method of communication that uses the aid of another person for physical and emotional support.

Flapping

The movement of the hand and forearm by a child or adult with autism that mimics a wave but occurs due to overstimulation, either physical or emotional.

Free Appropriate Public Education (FAPE)
Programs for education that meet a student's needs with the provision of adequate support.

Gluten-free, casein-free diet (GFCF)
A diet used by many parents of children on the autism spectrum. The diet excludes all gluten and casein products.

High-functioning autism (HFA)
A form of autism that is much less disabling as an individual has verbal ability and varying degrees of social understanding. IQ will be measured at seventy or above.

Imaginative play
The ability to play with objects using imagination. For example, toy cars, people, and houses can be a town in which an entire scenario is played out.

Inclusive
A term used interchangeably with mainstreaming. Refers to a child with a disability having access to the same classroom as if he were not disabled.

Individual Education Plan (IEP)
An official plan, written on a yearly basis, that is developed at a meeting with parents, teachers, therapists, and other experts involved in a disabled child's education.

Individuals with Disabilities Education Act (IDEA)
A United States congressional act that dictates all the rights children with disabilities have in order to receive full educational benefits from public schools.

IQ (intelligence quotient)
The number that is considered a standard for measuring a person's intelligence and capacity for understanding.

Least restrictive environment (LRE)
An educational term referring to the classroom or environment a student attends daily that provides the least amount of restriction to ensure safety and the most social and educational interaction.

Licensed clinical social worker (LCSW)
A mental-health professional licensed by each state to help individuals and families.

Low-functioning autism (LFA)
A more severe form of autism with IQ measuring at below seventy.

Meltdown
The total loss of behavioral control by a person with autism.

Neuro-immune dysfunction syndrome (NIDS)
The possible connection between neuro-immune and/or autoimmune dysfunction and conditions such as autism, ADD, Alzheimer's, ALS, CFS/CFIDS, MS, and other immune-mediated diseases.

Not otherwise defined (NOD)
Often appears with a diagnosis by a psychologist. This is a term that is used when a disorder is present but it does not fall into a specific definition within the diagnostic manuals.

Not otherwise specified (NOS)
Used as a footnote on a diagnosis when the disorder is vague in many ways (usually seen as PDD-NOS). It is considered a "catch-all" diagnosis and is often not accepted as a valid diagnosis by insurance companies.

Obsessive-compulsive disorder (OCD)
A disorder in which a person is obsessed with unwanted thoughts and feels the need to act out compulsive behaviors.

Occupational therapist or occupational therapy (OT)
A therapist who works with a patient to improve fine motor skills as well as developing solutions for practical day-to-day living as deficits are accommodated.

Parallel play
Playing beside another child, but playing independently and not interacting with that child.

Physical therapist or physical therapy (PT)
A therapist or therapy that works to increase the functionality of gross motor skills.

Picture exchange communication system (PECS/PCS)
A communication tool that uses photographs and/or drawings to replace words for language.

Receptive speech
Hearing spoken language from another person and deciphering it into a meaningful mental picture or thought pattern, which is understood and then used by the recipient.

Rett syndrome (RS)
A disorder on the autism spectrum. Rett syndrome is a genetic neurological disorder seen almost exclusively in females and found in a variety of racial and ethnic groups worldwide. It is characterized by apparently normal or near normal development until six to eighteen months of life. A period of temporary stagnation or regression follows, during which the child loses communication skills and purposeful use of the hands.

Selective serotonin reuptake inhibitor (SSRI)

A group of medications used for depression, anxiety, and the control of obsessive-compulsive behaviors, including Prozac, Zoloft, Paxil, and Luvox.

Self-contained

In reference to special education, it refers to schools or classrooms containing only a special-needs population.

Sensory overload

The reaction a child with autism has when more senses are being stimulated than she has the ability to process.

Service animal

An animal that is trained to work with and meet the needs of a disabled person.

Splinter skill

This is a highly refined skill accomplished by a child or adult with autism. Other skills may be below typical age level but one or two skills, such as music or computer programming, may be far above average.

Tic

A brief, repetitive, purposeless, nonrhythmic, involuntary movement or sound. Tics that produce movement are called "motor tics," while tics that produce sound are called "vocal tics" or "phonic tics." Tics tend to occur in bursts or "bouts."

Tourette's Syndrome (TS)

Also known as Tourette Syndrome or Tourette's disorder, this is a fairly common childhood-onset condition that may be associated with features of many other conditions. This syndrome is characterized by "tics."

Treatment and Education of Autistic and Related Communication Handicapped Children (TEACCH)

A method of teaching children with communication deficits that encourages communication with picture boards or other assistive devices.

Williams Syndrome

A disorder on the autism spectrum. Williams Syndrome is typically characterized by elfin face, dental problems, characteristic stenotic cardiovascular problems (narrowing of the blood vessels) and hypercalcemia (excessive calcium in the blood.) People with Williams Syndrome also have a characteristic tendency to approach strangers indiscriminately.

Additional Resources

The American Academy of Child and Adolescent Psychiatry
3615 Wisconsin Ave. NW
Washington, DC 20016-3007
202-966-7300
🖰 *www.aacap.org*

The American Academy of Child and Adolescent Psychiatry provides important information as a public service to assist parents and families in their most important roles.

Autism Research Institute
4182 Adams Avenue
San Diego, CA 92116
619-563-6840 (fax)
🖰 *www.autism.com*

The Autism Research Institute (ARI), a nonprofit organization, was established in 1967. ARI is primarily devoted to conducting research, and to disseminating the results of research, on the causes of autism and on methods of preventing, diagnosing, and treating autism and other severe behavioral disorders of childhood. They provide information based on research to parents and professionals throughout the world.

Autism Society

4340 East-West Highway, Suite 350

Bethesda, MD 20814

301-657-0881 or 1-800-3AUTISM

🖰 *www.autism-society.org*

ASA has over 200 chapters in nearly every state reaching out to individuals with autism and their families with information, support, and encouragement.

Autism Speaks

New York

2 Park Avenue

11th Floor

New York, NY 10016

212-252-8584

Princeton

1060 State Road, 2nd Floor

Princeton, NJ 08540

609-228-7310

Los Angeles

5455 Wilshire Boulevard

Suite 2250

Los Angeles, CA 90036

323-549-0500

🖰 *www.autismspeaks.org*

Autism Speaks is the largest autism science and advocacy organization in the U.S. It funds research into the causes, prevention, treatments, and a cure for autism. It also increases awareness of autism spectrum disorders, and advocates for the needs of individuals with autism and their families.

The BHARE Foundation

523 Newberry

Elk Grove, IL 60007

847-352-7678

⌨ *www.bhare.org*

The Brenen Hornstein Autism Research & Education (BHARE) Foundation's top priority is to fund research that will lead to a cure for autism. Good summaries for parents are available along with information regarding project funding.

Children's Rights Council

8181 Professional Place, Suite 240

Landover, MD 20785

⌨ *www.crckids.org*

The Children's Rights Council (CRC) is a national nonprofit organization based near Washington, DC, that works to assure children meaningful and continuing contact with both their parents and extended family regardless of the parents' marital status.

Doug Flutie Jr. Foundation for Autism

P.O. Box 767

Framingham, MA 01701

508-270-8855 or 1-866-3AUTISM

⌨ *www.dougflutiejrfoundation.org*

The Doug Flutie Jr. Foundation for Autism supports families affected by autism spectrum disorders, and promotes awareness for the disorders. They fund organizations that provide direct services, grants, education, advocacy, and recreational opportunities for individuals with autism and their families.

Families for Early Autism Treatment (FEAT)
P.O. Box 255722
Sacramento, CA 95865-5722
🖰 *www.feat.org*

Families for Early Autism Treatment (FEAT) is a California-based organization with chapters in several states. Among other things, FEAT publishes one of the most comprehensive, informative, and activist newsletters in the autism community.

Federation of State Medical Boards of the United States, Inc.
P.O. Box 619850
Dallas, TX 75261-9850
817-868-4000
🖰 *www.fsmb.org*

The Federation of State Medical Boards (FSMB) website allows you to research any serious disciplinary actions or professional peer reviews against a physician you are considering for your child.

For Parents Only.com
🖰 *www.forparentsonly.com*

For Parents Only.com is a specialized search engine connecting parents and information.

Free Appropriate Public Education (FAPE)
🖰 *www.fapeonline.org*

The Free Appropriate Public Education (FAPE) site is intended to be a beginning point for research by parents, educators, state and federal staff members, and other interested parties on a wide range of issues involving disabilities and disability law.

From Emotions to Advocacy (FETA)

⌂ *www.fetaweb.com*

Wrightslaw: From Emotions to Advocacy: The Special Education Survival Guide by Pam and Pete Wright, is an excellent resource for special education information. Fetaweb.com is the companion website to WrightsLaw.com.

International Society for Augmentative and Alternative Communication (ISAAC)

    49 The Donway West, Suite 308

    Toronto, ON M3C 3M9 Canada

    416-385-0351

⌂ *www.isaac-online.org*

The International Society for Augmentative and Alternative Communication (ISAAC) is an organization devoted to advancing the field of augmentative and alternative communication (AAC). The Mission of ISAAC is to promote the best possible communication for people with complex communication needs.

KeepKidsHealthy.com

⌂ *www.keepkidshealthy.com*

Keep Kids Healthy is an excellent pediatric medicine website.

Lovaas Institute for Early Intervention
11500 West Olympic Boulevard, Suite 460
Los Angeles, CA 90064
310-914-5433
🖱 *www.lovaas.com*

The Lovaas Institute for Early Intervention is a research-based program that specializes in teaching children with autism, pervasive developmental disorders, and related developmental disabilities. The program provides services nationwide.

The Medicine Program
P.O. Box 515
Doniphan, MO 63935-0515
573-996-7300
🖱 *www.themedicineprogram.com*

The Medicine Program may be able to help you with medication expenses. This organization was established by volunteers dedicated to alleviating the plight of an ever-increasing number of patients who cannot afford their prescription medication.

The National Autistic Society
393 City Road
London, EC1V 1NG, United Kingdom
44 (0)20 7833 2299
🖱 *www.autism.org.uk*

The National Autistic Society (NAS) is the UK's foremost organization for people with autism and those who care for them, spearheading national and international initiatives and providing a strong voice for autism. The NAS works in many areas to help people with autism live their lives with as much independence as possible.

The National Dissemination Center for Children with Disabilities (NICHCY)

1825 Connecticut Ave. NW, Suite 700

Washington, DC 20009

800-695-0285

⊙ *www.nichcy.org*

The National Information Center for Children and Youth with Disabilities (NICHCY) provides information on disabilities and disability-related issues. This organization is dedicated to providing information to parents and caregivers of children with disabilities, including autism/PDD.

National Organization of Social Security Claimants' Representatives (NOSSCR)

560 Sylvan Ave.

Englewood Cliffs, NJ 07632

201-567-4228

⊙ *www.nosscr.org*

The National Organization of Social Security Claimants' Representatives (NOSSCR) has a referral service for claimants looking for a private attorney and Social Security benefit information and representation. They also have a caller hotline number for SSI children's benefits. The referral is free; the attorney will charge for the representation if the claim is successful.

The Neuro Immune Dysfunction Syndromes (NIDS)
Research Institute
888-540-4999
🖰 *www.nids.net*

The Neuro Immune Dysfunction Syndromes (NIDS) Research Institute is dedicated to increasing the public's awareness of the likely connection between neuro-immune and/or autoimmune dysfunction and conditions such as autism, ADD, Alzheimer's, ALS, CFS/CFIDS, MS, and other immune-mediated diseases. If your family has an autoimmune illness situation as well as autism, you will want to check this out.

No Child Left Behind
U.S. Department of Education
400 Maryland Ave. SW
Washington, DC 20202
800-872-5327
🖰 *http://ed.gov/nclb*

The No Child Left Behind website includes a simple overview of the legislation, key dates to remember, frequently asked questions, information about what is happening in states across the country, and more importantly, where you can go to learn more and become involved. The goal of No Child Left Behind is to create the best educational opportunities for our nation's children and to ensure that they have every opportunity to succeed. The new revised legislation should make it much more effective.

Patient-Centered Guides Autism Center
🖰 *www.patientcenters.com/autism*

The Patient-Centered Guides Autism Center is for families of those living with a pervasive developmental disorder. Much of the material here is for those in the middle of the autistic spectrum, particularly those with a diagnosis of PDD-NOS or Atypical PDD or those still trying to find a correct diagnosis. You can find articles and resources about PDDs, diagnosis, drug treatments, therapies, supplements, education, insurance, family life, other coping topics, and resources.

Social Security Administration
800-772-1213
🖱 *www.ssa.gov*

The Social Security Administration website.

WrightsLaw.com
🖱 *www.wrightslaw.com*

WrightsLaw.com is one of the most thorough websites regarding autism and special education. Parents, advocates, educators, and attorneys come to Wrightslaw for accurate, up-to-date information about special-education law and advocacy for children with disabilities.

Index

We Have
EVERYTHING®
on Anything!

The Everything® list spans a wide range of subjects, with more than 500 titles covering 25 different categories:

Business	History	Reference
Careers	Home Improvement	Religion
Children's Storybooks	Everything Kids	Self-Help
Computers	Languages	Sports & Fitness
Cooking	Music	Travel
Crafts and Hobbies	New Age	Wedding
Education/Schools	Parenting	Writing
Games and Puzzles	Personal Finance	
Health	Pets	